Man: The Book

D1281847

MAN:

THE BOOK

A code of rules to be followed by a man amid the 21st Century's feminized society

is:

clay travis

chris shaw

dj harrison

josh townsend

kwo

hunter mccrary

CITADEL PRESS
Kensington Publishing Corp.
www.kensingtonbooks.com

CITADEL PRESS BOOKS are published by

Kensington Publishing Corp.
850 Third Avenue
New York, NY 10022

All Kensington titles, imprints, and distributed lines are available at special
quantity discounts for bulk purchases for sales promotions, premiums,
fund-raising, educational, or institutional use. Special book excerpts or
customized printings can also be created to fit specific needs. For details,
write or phone the office of the Kensington special sales manager:
Kensington Publishing Corp., 850 Third Avenue, New York, NY 10022,
attn: Special Sales Department; phone 1-800-221-2647.

First printing: February 2008

10   9   8   7   6   5   4   3   2   1

Printed in the United States of America

Library of Congress Control Number: 2007937044

ISBN-13: 978-0-8065-2871-7
ISBN-10: 0-8065-2871-0

When a book raises your spirit, and inspires you with noble and manly thoughts, seek for no other test of its excellence. It is good, and made by a good workman.
—Jean de La Bruyère

The Man Manifesto

Manhood is under assault. Where once men of all races, creeds, and continents could rest assured that such things as competitions with winner and losers, fondness for the voluptuous bodies of women, and widespread verbal and physical pummelings were accepted and celebrated, now we have musical chairs with the same number of children as chairs, are instructed to keep our eyes trained upon the floor in the presence of attractive women lest our eyes seem lecherous and are subjected to "put-up" contests as opposed to put-downs. A feminized society instructs us to abandon all precepts that our thoughts, desires, and delights are any different at all from those of a woman. Do this and we are bestowed the title of society's flaccid favorite, the metrosexual. The newly favored man is not really a man at all, but a hairless, effeminate, germ-fearing, meatless-eating, exfoliating, wristband-wearing woman of the worst order. We as men are told that we must embrace the sacred feminine in ourselves, even if it doesn't actually exist, and become the very quintessence of women, plus penises. This situation is untenable. Put plainly, a man divided against himself cannot stand.

Man: The Book comes as men across the world cling to the last vestiges of our masculinity. Forget global warming, the war on terror, and the possibility of avian flu. All of these events combined could not equal the pain of the slow drip of manhood's path to obscurity. We six authors of this book have taken our stand on the shores of masculinity, and woe unto anyone who continues to paddle (with arm floaties) along the fervent surf of the feminine onslaught. We see you there with shaved legs, no underarm hair, and a face so clean shaven you could still suckle on your mother's teat without raising her ire. We see you . . . and we can't stand you.

Within these pages you will find nothing less than the key to life. Follow the rules of *Man: The Book* and shortly you will find yourself afloat on a sea of happiness unlike any you have known before. Women who previously had believed they wanted a larger Adam's-appled version of themselves as a companion will throw themselves at your feet. Your forty-time will decrease and your bench-press will increase. You may even get drafted. It is entirely possible that you will kill an animal and eat it raw, like the great and ancient predator you are. Slowly, the world around you will change, revealing all its many competitions, voluptuous women, and physical and verbal pummelings that you had forgotten you so richly enjoyed. We have seen the power of the 975 *Man: The Book* rules in this book.* It has changed all our lives. We beseech you, join the *Man: The Book* movement and discover the freedom of truly being a man.

---

*Like all great religions, our share of contradictory advice is offered within these pages. The authors of *Man: The Book* humbly request that you treat these contradictions in the same manner as you might treat contradictory advice in the great religions of the world. Namely, you may either (a) ignore all conflicts and pretend they do not exist, (b) rigidly adhere to one of the rules while ridiculing the very idea that someone might believe the other, or (c) embark upon a war of mutually assured annihilation.

If you don't, the world will continue its slovenly slouch toward the eradication of masculinity. Until, mark our words, one young boy will be born fifteen years hence and, quite simply, his testes will never descend. *Ever.* Don't let this boy be your son/girl.

Contents

I.

Bars and Restaurants

Always do sober what you said you'd do drunk.
That will teach you to keep your mouth shut.
—Ernest Hemingway

The water was not fit to drink. To make it
palatable, we had to add whiskey. By diligent
effort, I learned to like it.
—Sir Winston Churchill

In ancient times, men proved their self-worth on fields of battle with axes and arrows laced with fire and poison. If you beheaded someone, you also got his wife, daughters, and his oxcart. It was a simple yet fulfilling life (provided, of course, that you kept your head and did not die of scurvy or syphilis). But now men live in the twenty-first century and the bar has replaced the battlefield as the point of conquest. Sure, some guys pick up women at coffee shops, vintage clothing stores, and haberdasheries. These are not men. These are vultures sent to comb the edges of the battlefield. In ancient times, they would have been the men in charge of driving swords into the other men who were already mortally wounded and clinging to the edges of life. These men still masturbate to Victoria's Secret catalogs and run their fingers along frilly lace bras when they are in department stores. You do not want to be one of these men. (Of course, every man can feel comfortable running his hands along frilly lace thongs so long as they are sizes 0, 2, or 4. Okay, okay, and if you are a black man, sizes 6, 8, and 10 too.) No, real men fight real battles at the bar. Win and all womankind will spread their legs before you. Lose, and you'll be relegated to hitting on chicks at the sushi counter in Harris Teeter grocery stores. Not that there's anything wrong with hitting on chicks at the sushi counter, but come on, how many times can you giggle and say, "Oh my god, do you like California rolls, too?"

Just as men trained themselves in archery, sword-fighting, ax-swinging, and disemboweling on the verdant

2

plains of old England, so too, must you train yourself on the oaken tables of the bar. You have to know what not to drink, what not to wear, and how to use gay men to your advantage. (Gay men are like the cavalry of the modern bar.) Soon, like Neo in *The Matrix*, all around you the bar will spin with exquisite slowness. That girl in the top with breasts that resemble sacks of sawdust mixed with Elmer's Glue-All? That guy in the camouflage will leave with her. That exquisite knockout who can barely stand because she is so drunk and is wearing high heels? Place yourself correctly and you can bump into her and pretend it's her fault. She'll believe you. Then she'll go home and screw you for so long you won't be able to touch your penis in the morning when you piss. You'll see this all developing around you in super slow-motion. We promise you.

Not every man may become the One but, with effort, every man can become a warrior. Otherwise, don't listen to us, and there will be many nights when you trudge home with a woman who resembles a battle-ax affixed to your hip. She will be giggling and you will feel her belly rolling alongside you. Later as you rabbit-hump her with wild abandon while she absently chews on a Tootsie Roll, you may be tempted to cry. And this will be a good night. Other nights, you will go home with your guy friends and have masturbation races utilizing old Madonna posters from 1986 as excitement. Trust us, grasshopper, read on and we will show you the way to move on the bar battlefield.

1. No matter how crowded the bar is, if a man asks you for your table so that he can start an arm-wrestling tournament, you must relinquish it immediately.

2. When ordering drinks, insist that the weakest drinker of the group get the first round. Drink it, then wander around the bar until you see everyone else on empty. Then the second weakest drinker must buy. This is called the Drinking Darwinism Theory.

3. If the bathroom line is too long, don't be afraid to think outside the box. Appropriate alternatives include the sink, trash cans, beer bottles, and the floor. Peeing is basically allowed anywhere but on yourself.

4. The more shots you take past 2:00 A.M., the less ass you will get that night. Believe us.

5. If Patrick Swayze is the bouncer of the bar and/or it's made of all wood, by all means go inside and have a drink.

6. Every man has a bar which he refers to only as "the bar." When asked by someone else, "*What* bar?" one must respond, "*The* bar." Generally this bar is dirty, inhabited by rednecks and thugs (not women), and, most important, cheap.

7. If another guy wants to fight you and he says in a very calm voice, "I think we should take this outside," do not ever go outside. He will kill you.

8. Being able to outdrink someone trumps athletic ability. Athleticism is God given, boozing is a learned trait.

9. Vodka and cranberry may be ordered for your own consumption only if the bar is so dark no one can tell your drink is pink.

10.

Girl	Boy	Man
Amaretto sour	Whiskey sour	Straight bourbon
Hard cider	Light beer	Bitter stout
Mudslide	White Russian*	Black Russian

11. When at a restaurant, never order a dish with the word *medley* in it.

12. If you arrive before your friends at a bar, feel free to fake a cell phone call. Smile and say something witty if necessary. Feel free to refake a cell phone call every ten minutes until someone actually arrives. If no one ever arrives, reconsider your life.

13. When walking into a bar, always suck in gut and expand chest until you confirm that you are not the fattest man in the bar. When confirmed, exhale.

14. Light beers may always be consumed; diet sodas may never be consumed.

15. You are obligated to get weekend drunk on Saint Patrick's Day and Cinco de Mayo.

*Permitted for men in the act of watching, discussing, or thinking about *The Big Lebowski*.

16. When you travel to another city to visit a friend, consider it a free invitation to get twice as drunk as you do in your home city.

17. Every man should have at least one drinking story that ends in the phrase, "and then I woke up with my pants off." However, if this story also includes the phrases, "And then Richard Simmons . . ." or "And then Balki from *Perfect Strangers* . . ." keep that one to yourself.

18. If you are playing either quarters or beer pong and the quarter or Ping-Pong ball lands on the floor, anytime someone mentions germs, he is forced to wear a headband for the remainder of the night. If your friend is already wearing a headband, make him take off his accompanying wristbands and punch him in the nose. He shouldn't be your friend, anyway.

19. If you lose a drinking game to a girl, leave the party and contemplate self-gelding.

20. When eating at a restaurant, if another man at your table orders an alcoholic drink, you are required to order a stronger drink than the one he just ordered. This should be followed by a look of pity directed at the other man, a chuckle, then a headshake.

21. Never write any type of invitation that includes the term BYOB. Beer is the nectar of men and deserves to be spelled in its entirety.

22. Whenever you encounter an unidentified man on the street, at work, or at a bar or club, immediately assess whether you could kick his ass (comparing forearm sizes is a good indicator). Adjust behavior accordingly.

23. *General Barfight Rule*: The bigger they are, the harder they punch.

24. If you are about to slather yourself in cologne before going out, just remember it's mostly deer piss.

25. When seeing a bachelorette party, fervently hitting on the bride-to-be is a must. Then work your way down the bridal party ladder until you get laid. Take an average 1–10 rating of the girl you hook up with from your friends, round up, and that is the number of shots you are owed the next night out. (The bride is an automatic bottle of champagne.) This game is called "Shots and Ladders."

26. It's always okay to remind a bouncer who won't let you into a club that you make more money than he does . . . so long as you don't really value your teeth.

27. When holding your beer bottle at the bar, do not turn it into a phallic symbol by fingering it or stroking it subconsciously, especially in a group of other men. From across the bar, this makes you look really gay. Grip it like a man and swill.

28. Saturday night at two in the morning, some guy's always at the bar in a tie. His schedule is so busy he couldn't have spent the thirty seconds it would have taken to pull off that tie? Wait until he's checking his fancy watch and then grab his tie and choke him to within an inch of his life.

29. Going to the drunk tank is the equivalent of getting caught in one of those Indian rabbit snares. Just chew your leg off, escape, and keep drinking, you pussy.

30. The next day after a party, the person who threw up the night before has to drink a beer casserole. This consists of at least four of the leftover beers combined in one pitcher. This will teach them to waste good booze.

31. Upon entering a bar, always imagine the theme song from *The Good, the Bad, and the Ugly* playing in the background. Anyone who looks like he has never seen the movie is now instantly your enemy. If you have never seen the movie, you have made a good investment in buying this book.

32. A good steak is like a good pussy. Raw, hairless, and juicier than all git'-out.

33. Eat your pizza *and* your fucking bread crusts. Wasting the crust is like not finishing the last of your beer because it's warm. Besides, if crust is the worst thing you've ever put in your mouth, you're not a man, anyway. Sack up.

34. If your stall doesn't have a lock or a door, fuck it, take that shit anyway. Any man who stares or otherwise encroaches on the deed is in the wrong bathroom.

35. A man must possess a minimum of two ways to open a beer bottle without a bottle opener. And your male friend named Taylor's way of asking the bartender *isn't* one of them.

36. Here's a good way to tell if you are too drunk to keep drinking: If the smell of your own vomit makes you gag and nearly vomit again, then have another drink: you are not nearly wasted enough.

37. When out to eat and the waitress asks you "mild, medium, or hot," the answer should always be "hotter'n hell!" If you are less than a month removed from triple bypass surgery, it is acceptable to order medium. Never under any circumstances order mild; you don't want your order to be confused with that of your four-year-old niece.

38. A salad does not constitute a meal, unless it's a meat salad, where a meat salad is defined as a pile of (preferably freshly killed) raw meat.

39. In order to eliminate time-wasting decision-making and keep the line moving, at a barbecue, when asked if you would like a "[blank] or a [blank]," always answer authoritatively, "Both. And a beer." For instance:

> Question: Hot dog or hamburger?
> Answer: Both, and get me a fucking beer.

This answer may need to be adjusted based on the options:

> Question: Hot dog, hamburger, chicken, or steak?
> Answer: All four. Now. Raw. And bring me a fucking beer.

40. If a sandwich anywhere costs more than a steak at Outback, you may not purchase it.

41. When eating at a seafood restaurant with your girl, it's always fun to use the crab claws in an inappropriate fashion. Try pinching her nipples with them every time the waiter comes around, or tell the waiter, "This isn't the first time she's had crabs." Basically, don't fail to use a crab when you have the opportunity.

42. No man shall make less than three trips when dining in an all-you-can-eat Chinese buffet. If any two men surpass your intake of Chinese for the meal, they have the automatic right to tag-team your girlfriend until you finish your third plate.

43. When the short-skirted, hot, nineteen-year-old waitress asks you if you want Parmesan cheese with your Italian meal, with your answer (which, by the way, is yes) you may include subtle or nonsubtle indications that you would be happy to sprinkle her with white droplets later that evening in the coat closet, also.

44. If you have to pass gas in a bar, go ahead and fart. Immediately blame the smell on the first ugly person you see.

45. The hierarchy at a bar is determined by ability to slam a beer. If you can polish one off in under eight seconds, the other bar patrons should show you a level of respect on par with that of professional athletes. If you can accomplish the feat in under three seconds, you are a god and others should not look you directly in the eye.

46. If two men go to a bar or restaurant together, under no circumstances should you both go to the bathroom at the same time. Doing this will automatically flag you as a homosexual to every single woman in the establishment.

47. *Meeting women in bars:* If you use a pickup line on a woman at a bar sincerely, you are an idiot and it won't work. If you use a pickup line on a woman with the hope that she will find it funny and hook up with you anyway, chances are it's not funny and it won't work. The solution: If you're really attractive, just act dumb and you'll wake up next to a naked woman. If you're rich, just flash your money clip at her. If you're not, then pretend you're rich. If you can't do that, you're screwed—what are you doing at a bar, anyway?

48. If a hot waitress leaves you her number on the tab, you must hook up with her. No excuses.

49. If you have ever kicked a bouncer's ass, stop while you're ahead. Feel free to frequent that bar and act like a nice guy. Offer him a drink.

50. When out drinking with the boys, quote humorous lines from movies, TV shows, and life experiences regardless of how many times they have been told before. If you are in this group listening, laugh as hard as you did the first time you heard it. If it was funny then, it is funny now.

51. If someone goes to buy a round and he lacks the ability to get to the front of the bar in a reasonable amount of time, feel free to lap him and buy the next round. If lapped, this means your friend has to stay at the bar and buy the next three rounds in succession.

52. Once you have been safely restrained from an altercation at the bar, feel free to talk as much trash as possible.

53. If you ever bring anything to a party or picnic, the leftovers are yours. You paid for them, and for the gas to go get them. Hold receipts if necessary.

54. When traveling to a new city, always act as if you know exactly where the cool bar is to go. If it sucks, tell everyone that you must be there on the wrong night of the week.

55. Make out with a random girl on the dance floor of a bar at least biannually.

56. If you call a waiter *maître d'*, saw at your wrist with the butter knife, then order two shots of Jack or Jim: one to drink, and the other to pour in your gaping vagina.

57. If you ever have a quickie with a waitress while she's at work, you have achieved male greatness. If it happens in the kitchen, tell your male friends so they never go to that place again.

58. Every meal is a competition: eat fast and if you can still move at the end, it's time for seconds.

59. You should learn to be at least decent in all games played at a bar (darts, pool, shuffleboard, Golden Tee, foosball, etc.). However, if another man you have not previously met challenges you to a duel in any of the aforementioned games, and drinks or money are involved, do not accept the challenge. This man is an expert and will verily expose your lack of aptitude in bar sports, embarrassing you in public in the process.

60. Coming out victorious in a life-or-death struggle with a vicious predator (e.g., grizzly bears, Siberian tigers, great white sharks, or other sundry deadly animals) gives you automatic front of the line status at a keg party.

61. You absolutely may not use the word *sip* when referring to beer or whiskey. The words *chug*, *slam*, and *shoot* are preferred.

62. Drink a beer while pissing to simulate the gist of the expression "It's going right through me."

63. Always make certain that you are not the best-dressed man at any club, bar, or social event that includes women. If you are, women will automatically assume you are gay and so will gay men. In fact, you might actually be gay.

64. If two men are at a restaurant together and one man is in the bathroom, then the other man may not order for him. The rules are clear on this: if he misses the waiter, he doesn't eat.

65. Never eat dinner at a restaurant alone. An exception to this rule exists for dinners eaten at the bar and not within the city limits of the city in which you live.

66. If you ever get caught with a fake ID, offer the bouncer a blow job for its return. If he says yes, run. It was probably a gay bar, and if it wasn't, you wanted no parts of what was inside. Your ID will be gone, but your anus will be safe for one more night at least.

67. Never, ever, drink the free coffee they put out for truckers at adult bookstores. This is like pouring liquid herpes down your throat.

68. When two sissies (or frat boys) fight at a bar, inevitably it will end up like a grappling war. Not a crowd-pleaser. To avoid this, separate them, take them outside, and tie their wrists together like in MJ's *Beat It* video. Slap them both and give them plastic knives. Collect a $50 stipend for the bouncer as a referee, ensuring they will fight until one bleeds or submits, or the bouncer will beat their asses while lashed together, donning only plastic cutlery for defense. Either way, it'll be hilarious.

69. Eat nine out of every ten meals in front of the television. Of those nine, eat at least three while standing.

70. At least once in your life, tell someone at a bar to "Eat shit and die." Then, turn around and walk away.

71. Potato chips are a perfectly acceptable meal.

72. Contrarily, a man may only eat berries if they are involved in sexual activity with whipped cream.

73. If you are bigger than everyone else in the room, you get the last sandwich/beer/french fry.

74. A man listens to techno music if and only if he is engaged in the act of pelvic thrusting a drunk, hot, and slutty girl. A man owns no techno music and does not enter a techno club unless he is sure of receiving sexual compensation for the emasculation.

75. Bathroom attendants are to be avoided in general; if made to feel guilty about not leaving a tip, pause directly in front of said attendant and straighten his bow tie. Even if it is already straight. Then stand alongside him for a minute or so waiting for a tip. If none is forthcoming, make a dismissive gesture in his direction and feel free to take a mint and call it even.

76. If you're allergic to something, keep it to yourself. Just pick it off and eat your goddamn food.

77. During World War II, Japanese soldiers used to place glass rods inside American men's penises and then chop up the rods. Yeah. Think about this the next time your girlfriend takes you out for sushi. You homo.

78. Getting so drunk that you soil yourself in your sleep is okay, but finding out a way to blame it on someone else is better.

79. At an event which involves a barbecue, all men must spend at least 50 percent of the time standing around the grill, regardless of weather. Topics of conversation are limited to the strength of the fire, sports, and milfs.

80. A man that lives alone must possess a microwave and a grill. An actual oven is optional.

81. Be suspicious of any bar with only one word as a name. Run in the other direction if the bar's name sounds like it could be the brand of your girlfriend's jeans.

82. The appropriate accompanying wine for any meal is, surprisingly, beer.

83. If a man makes a fist with his thumb inside, feel very comfortable that he is not capable of hurting you in a bar fight.

84. A man may order a smoothie on two occasions: (1) when there is actually a woman fellating him while he stands at the smoothie counter ordering. Actually, screw that, there is only one.

85. Everybody has one lightweight friend who gets drunk after two beers, no matter how often he drinks. This man may always be referred to as "twosie." If you have more than one friend who can be referred to as twosie, you may all be referred to as this: a boy band in training.

86. At a bar, a man never needs to concern himself with another man's having or not having a seat at the table. However, if a hot girl wants to join the table, your lap is always available.

87. You may never wear a sleeveless shirt to a bar or restaurant. Even if you have Hulk Hogan-esque pythons. Note: This rule, like many other rules, does not apply in Mexico or the Caribbean, as, in either place, you may also feel comfortable pulling out your penis and slapping it on the table in time to "Yankee Doodle Dandy" for the amusement of everyone.

88. If you break a glass while drinking at a party or bar, you are either too drunk to be trusted with glassware anymore or your puny muscles are unable to firmly grasp the smooth surface of the glass. In both cases, you have to drink the rest of the night through a straw to prevent any further loss of beer or alcohol.

89. Any man who attempts to order a veggie pizza for other men may be drawn and quartered. Feel free to cook his body parts and use them as meat-toppings.

90. Eating more than everyone else at the table is an honor and should be acknowledged by any other men eating with you. A simple comment such as, "Man, you really went to work on those Cheetos! Nice work!" will suffice.

91. At no point does any man who is cooking outdoors have to consider dietary restrictions of his guests, such as veganism, vegeterianism, South Beach diet, or any other trendy weight-loss diet we are not aware of. If you don't want to eat a juicy flame-broiled burger, then don't go to a goddamn barbecue.

92. Stay out of all Southern bar fights until you have proved yourself in at least one Ultimate Fighting Championship.

93. In a bar, feel free to bring a beer with you to the urinal, but not to the shitter.

94. A drinking game may not be played by two men alone. Just drink.

95. No matter how much you might want to do it, having sex with a girl in the middle of a crowded bar is an activity reserved for drunk, mulleted rednecks. And Kobayashi.

96. As impossible as you may find it to believe, women actually go to dance clubs to dance . . . with other women. Conversely, you would not dance with another man if your life depended on it. This is one of life's great ironies.

97. If you take a woman home from a club, bar, grocery store, bowling alley, or fast-food restaurant and have sex with her, you are not the first guy she has done this with. Seriously, stop strutting and prepare for painful urination.

II.

Women

I'll promise to go easier on drinking and to get to bed earlier, but not for you, fifty thousand dollars, or two hundred and fifty thousand dollars will I give up women. They're too much fun.
—Babe Ruth

There is a 100 percent chance that if every woman on earth knew what goes through your mind on a daily basis, no one would ever sleep with you again. And you might be in prison. Except, of course, for the girls with daddy issues. Those girls will still sleep with you even while you slap them in the face with a limp penis and end up giving them several iterations of the clap. Nevertheless it is a scientifically proven fact that the only thing men think about more often than having sex with a woman is having sex with multiple women at the same time. Fortunately, it is only upon rigorous adherence to the rules of *Man: The Book* that you even have a chance to fulfill this multiple-women fantasy. That's because, despite what your friend who wears turtlenecks, scarves, and wristbands likes to say, women don't like men who are pussies, either. In fact, most women hate other women. So why would they want to hang out with a guy who envies their slit?

But not everyone gets this. In fact, right now there is also a 100 percent chance you have a guy friend with a girlfriend who sucks (figuratively, not literally). This guy friend does all sorts of things that make you want to shoot yourself in the penis with a nail gun. He brags about their heavy petting, shows off the hickey on his collarbone as if it were the equivalent of taking an exploding shell on the beaches of Normandy, and says things like, "I don't even really think about sex with her. We just cuddle and talk." No matter how many times you've told your friend that grown men shouldn't still describe their sexual experiences utilizing the bases from baseball, it doesn't take. "Slid into third last night," your buddy will say while nodding his head in a cocky manner and pumping his fist. Your buddy is so busy self-gelding himself that he will listen to no reason. Inevitably, trust us, this girl is getting banged by a guy with a twelve-inch cock who can't even spell *cuddle*. She's probably even making videos with him where she covers all the bases . . . and then some. Inevitably, this same friend is going to come home one night and say something like, "I knew when I could get four fingers inside her it was a bad sign. She's no virgin. That bitch." Then this friend will cry. You have no obligation to hug him, but you do have an obligation to pass him this book open to page 10. Tell him to read and stop tweezing his eyebrows while he twirls his hips to Barbra Streisand classics. Then go bang chicks.

98. If you are with a group of men and you see a woman's thong peeping out of her jeans like a timid meerkat looking out of its hole for predators, you are obligated to bring the aforementioned thong to the attention of all men present. Then comment on how badly you want to bone her.

99. Fish are like women: they can sense desperation. So eat breakfast before you go fishing and jerk off before you go to the bar.

100. If a hot girl breaks up with you, she immediately becomes twice as hot, and your new life goal becomes getting her in bed again. Look deep within your soul: you know it's true.

101. Feel free to stare at a belly-button ring, exposed thong, fake boobs, or lower-back tattoo (a.k.a the bull's-eye). Ogle if necessary. That is what they are there for.

102. Anything you say or promise to a woman while drunk is completely inadmissible and cannot be enforced.

103. A sister's cleavage is always fair game, unless it is your own sister.

104. If your girlfriend's name ends in *i* (Candi, Kelli, Randi, Christi), multiply by five the number of men she says she has slept with, to derive the actual number. This will still be low, but it will be closer to the truth.

105. If a girl is conversant about the term *airtight*, do not introduce her to your mother.

106. If you ever get married, your wife gets pregnant, and you have a son, teach him how to throw and catch a football. If you have a daughter, divorce your wife and leave the state, for she has failed you.

107. Lots of men screw ugly women; this is how ugly women end up with children. Do the world a favor and use a condom. Or cut to the humor chase and name your kid Cleft Palate.

108. If your girl fixes something you can't, the next time you have sex, make it doggy style. This will even it out.

109. Breakups with girlfriends can only occur after fights. Anyone who tells you otherwise is lying. If you need a breakup aid, friends can be encouraged and used to instigate said fights. For instance, one easy way to instigate a fight with your girlfriend is to have a friend give the change-pitcher signal in the presence of your current girlfriend when a hot chick walks by. It consists of tapping the right arm and raising one's eyebrows while pointing at the hot chick.

110. If you admit to having a favorite actress, you have to be able to respond, without thinking, when queried as to the status of nude scenes involving her. Specificity of body part nudity is required. If either you do not know this or your favorite actress is not naked in any films, you need a new favorite actress or none at all.

111. Some women exist solely to break slumps. Among them: The "Stocking Stuffer": A fat girl wearing tube socks causing her calf to pour over the top, a.k.a. the boiling

pot. This same female could also be "Baking Bread," when her cankles pour out of her shoe, resembling doughy, leavened bread rising. Like breaking the glass for a fire extinguisher, be careful.

112. If a girl is embarrassed to have hooked up with you afterward, it means it was a good night for you.

113. Women may play football with you only when they are hot, it involves two-hand touch, and they are wearing bikinis.

114. Sex is not and has never been free.

115. Periods equal no sex, but no babies. A fair trade.

116. Know the age of sexual consent in your home state and at least 50 percent of contiguous border states.

117. If any man (whether you know him or not) asks you to see the naked pictures you took of an ex-girlfriend, you are obligated to show them to him. If another man asks you to see the naked pictures of your current girlfriend or wife, you are obligated to kill him with your bare hands.

118. No matter how bad the service, leave a hot waitress at least a 25 percent tip.

119. Never feel bad about staring at a girl's breasts when she is wearing a white tank top and it rains. After all, God made it rain.

120. When confined in closed quarters such as an elevator or subway, it is perfectly normal to account for all women in the area and to rank them in order of who you would sleep with first, if you were the last survivors on earth. Upon further reflection, this is not limited to confinement in closed quarters, but should occur in any geographic area where you and more than one female are present. Candidates cannot be excluded on the basis of age, weight, disability, or any other characteristic— the survival of the world may depend on your selection.

121. Every man has picked out at least one spot in his room where he knows he could set up a camera if the girl he brings home is drunk enough to agree.

122. If your girlfriend names your rod, keep this a secret. Your friends don't want to hear stories about "Puffy the Vampire Layer."

123. When passing a woman while driving, you must stare at the woman relentlessly until you determine her hotness level. If she is hot, a honk may be required, followed by the rearview mirror stare until she is out of sight.

124. Every man is allowed one night of rampant sex with a woman far below his normal standards, also known as "slump-busting." After a night such as this, you should use the following saying as your fellow men mock you, "Even if you can eat a steak every day, sometimes a man just wants a bologna sandwich." This excuse is acceptable only once. If you remain in

a slump, it might just mean you are godawfully ugly, in which case the slump is really just your life.

125. If it gets you into bed with a girl, it isn't a lie.

126. Deep down, each woman is aware that she is a little bit crazy. Exploit this to your advantage.

127. We're fine with women's equality, just ensure that when you go out, she picks up exactly half of everything consumed. If she refuses, do not budge. Have her arrested if necessary.

128. If a girl has a ferret as a pet, do not date her. If she has a bird, demand that she free him.

129. A man always remembers both the hookup he most regrets and the hookup he most wants to repeat.

130. Nudge and point freely when two attractive girls do anything close to kissing (holding hands and touching hair counts). When it is two unattractive girls, you are allowed to look, but that will not warrant the nudge and point.

131. If the girl won't take off her bra during a backrub, then you aren't getting any sex. Cease and desist all movements, and open a can of beer.

132. When watching women at a strip club, do not comment upon whether their breasts are real or fake; what's important is that they are bare.

133. If your ex ever dates anyone bigger than you, when you see them out together inquire, "How does my dick taste?" Actually, no, just think it or you will get pummeled.

134. No woman will ever fulfill all of your needs as Daisy Duke once did; accept this as best you can.

135. If your girl has a nipple ring, she has the obligation to show at least one of your friends, mainly for proof. Know that said friend will most likely masturbate later that evening to this image.

136. It's always okay to point out that lesbian women always seem to date girls who look like really wimpy guys. Unless you are a really wimpy guy, at which point you might get beaten up by a lesbian.

137. If a girl can bench more than you, you have two options:

    (1) Cut and run, provided she can't also beat you up, or

    (2) Give her your boxers and start wearing her panties.

138. It's okay and normal to fantasize about the mail girl at your office even if she isn't that hot.

139. If you've been wondering all these years, Mary Poppins *was* doable.

140. Wearing a WWJD [What Would Jesus Do] bracelet is a good way to ensure you never get laid.

141. Give up explaining to women that other men are nice to them because they want to have sex. For whatever reason, women refuse to accept this.

142. Treat all sorority houses as a 24-hour buffet: Always go back for seconds or thirds, and always wear a bib.

143. If you can play any song on a guitar for longer than a minute, then do so with your door open in full view of chicks. Have a semipained look on your face and stare at a corner in the room. At the end, sigh and say, "Just wish I could think of how to finish it . . ." If *anyone* takes the bait, you will inevitably lay her.

144. Be extremely leery of homophones. For example:

    Phat ass: When the string of a thong hides seductively nestled between two nicely sculpted ass cheeks. Pursue with reckless abandon.

    Fat ass: When granny panties somehow form a thong after being sucked in by the vortex of two bags of cottage cheese she calls an ass. Avoid.

145. If you are lucky enough to have any hot chicks working in your office, hit on them mercilessly, holding nothing back. Feel free to proposition sex so long as they are your subordinates. If raised in some sort of sexual harassment complaint, obviously deny everything.

146. Rather than be concerned with whether a woman's breasts are fake, refuse to adopt the word *fake* at all. For instance, you don't continually refer to a man with

an artificial heart as having a fake heart. Instead, follow this rule: If something is inside the skin, it's real.

147. Church is a great place to meet chicks so long as you have a favorite Bible verse. However, if you don't have a favorite Bible verse, don't try and fake it. As much as you might wish Jesus had said, "Come sit on my face and let me play with your chest midgets," throwing a Matthew 24 at the end doesn't really do the trick.

148. If you're ever standing in the bathroom with your girlfriend and she says, "Could you pass me a tampon?" for the love of God do not look at her while she inserts the tampon.

149. Picking the right intern is very important. After all, you need to pick someone who is comfortable being aggressively sexually harassed. And that's not always easy to tell. Choose wisely and never put anything in email.

150. Words of advice an old man once told us, "When it's time to pick a secretary, always pick the chick with the biggest tits. After all, you can teach anyone to type but you can't teach anyone to have big tits." (Note: This was before fake breasts were as common as kids with autism.)

151. Next time your buddy makes out with a chick with a visibly masculine feature (large hands, wide shoulders, legs like cinder blocks, a neck that could be yoked

and used to plow), claim you saw her pissing at the urinal. Wait until he's really drunk and will believe you. Then pretend you have been waiting for the right time to tell him. Trust us, this will be fun.

152. Next time a buddy of yours is spending way too much time playing with a kid to impress his girlfriend who you hate, lean over to her and say, "He just loves kids." She'll grin and nod. Then continue, "Especially on all those videos he has of them naked in the bathtub."

153. Next time you go to France and you meet a hot chick, she's going to try and kiss you on each cheek. Turn your head so that your lips meet and try to slip her your tongue. Hey, it might work. And if it doesn't? Well, what have you lost?

154. Sometimes boob jobs don't work. For instance, we all know a woman who got fake boobs and now her breasts resemble sacks of Elmer's Glue-All and wood-chips. Don't ever tell your wife or girlfriend about this woman. After all, some people die taking showers. And you don't base your life around this fear, do you?

155. If you absolutely must have anal sex, go to a Promise-Keepers rally. Those girls may swear to be virgins but that means you can fuck them in the ass for days.

156. Any movie featuring Hugh Grant or Meg Ryan may only be watched in an attempt to take advantage of an emotionally vulnerable female. If you have ever watched those movies alone and enjoyed the experi-

ence, such enjoyment must never be spoken of, and any person to accuse you of this must be threatened with strangulation.

157. If a girl ever does something as brazen as approach you in a bar, take a lollipop out of your mouth, lick it, and put it back in your mouth, then there is absolutely no excuse for not hooking up with her.

158. Don't worry, girls, popping hymens is like popping zits. Well, maybe really bloody zits. Actually, we're sick now.

159. If you ever doubted women were weird, just remember this fact: They, like fish and fowl, have eggs. Yep, eggs. This is very underdiscussed. Worst of all, you can't even eat their eggs. And if they get fertilized, they end up costing you money. Talk about a bad deal.

160. When having sex with a much older woman, pull out and nut in her belly button, forming a pool in the depression. Tell her she is now the "Fountain of Youth" and she will never die.

161. If the last time you ever had sex with a girl was doggy style, then it was a good relationship . . . for you, at least.

162. When a girl is on the rag, "dipsticking" is not allowed, no matter how close she is until the red tide recesses. That's sick, dude, just beat off for a few days. And if, God forbid, you're one of those sick vampire fucks

who eats a girl out while she's on her period . . . well, there's really no hope for you.

163. *Always* remember the number of girls you told your girl you slept with. They *never* forget. This is probably the only lie you can never get out of.

164. Hitting on a chick in a hospital is about as low as you can go. Actually, hanging out just outside the abortion clinic is probably lower . . . but safer. After all, you know those chicks are healthy enough to screw.

165. Bad luck isn't breaking a mirror or seeing a black cat walk in front of you, it's losing your virginity to a chick with herpes.

166. When your girl-for-the-night is asleep, deftly wipe some of your BO under her nose or behind her ears. This is called rubber-stamping and will mark your territory for at least eighteen hours, more than enough time to decide whether you want to bang her again.

167. Pulling off a Wobbly H, a.k.a. the Spit Roast, is way less creepy if the other guy isn't staring into your eyes while he is pumping away at his end.

168. When a girl says you are only being nice because you want sex, go ahead and admit it. Then point out the dark circles under her eyes and all the stretch marks on her lower back. Follow this up by asking if you can have sex. She didn't like the change of scenery, did she?

169. Never beg for sex. Just pop in a porn and stare at her. She will get the point or leave. Either way, you are going to bust a nut. Bottom line is, never beg for anything that should be free.

170. The reason why women don't like porn is because they are jealous they can't fuck or look hot like porn stars. Offer to guide her through this nervosa with a happy heart. And make sure you duck, because the slap is coming.

171. Men like porn for the same reason women like romantic comedies: it's fantasy shit that will never happen. So if you have to throw away your porn, she has to throw away that crap, too.

172. Coming too early is like eating too fast; there is no such thing.

173. If you are ever in a position where you have to hold a girl's purse, then during said time you are more than entitled to stare, ogle, or otherwise comment on any hot chick in the vicinity, with unabashed lewdness.

174. When you ask a girl to count something say "Tally, ho!" in an English accent.

175. Irony is the fact that every girl loves those self-gelding Hugh Grant movies, yet he got caught cheating on his girlfriend with a hooker. The next time you get

caught doing the same, just say, "Hugh, all right? I learned it by watching Hugh!!" like in those drug commercials. You should get off scot-free.

176. A diamond ring is a very, very expensive Band-Aid.

177. Telling your girl you just gave her a "round of applause" instead of "the clap" will not make it any funnier . . . at least to her.

178. Going to a college with a 4:1 girl-to-guy ratio may not get your ass laid. Making her a drink with a 4:1 booze ratio has much better odds and is way cheaper.

179. Be familiar with honorary phrases. For instance, *pulling a wilt*: having sex with more than three girls in the same day. If you have done this, you probably should have written your own book rather than reading ours.

180. The more you feed a girl on a date, the less chance you have of her swallowing what really matters later on.

181. Tell your girl: anything you could have done yourself is not considered satisfying, such as TV dinners and hand jobs.

182. The next time your girl looks in the window at an expensive dress or jewelry and longingly sighs, find the next hot girl in a window and do the same thing. She will cut that shit right the fuck out.

183. If another guy agrees to kiss you just to see two girls get it on, by all means, go ahead . . . and kill him with your bare hands. Then have a threesome.

184. Libraries and hospitals are the two hardest places to pick up chicks. This is because women are usually sober and/or dying. At a library, wait in the self-help aisle until a hot chick walks by and then cry while you read some book called *What She Really Means: Understanding Women and Their Mangled Vaginas*. At a hospital, go straight for the rape victims and offer your protection. Cha-ching.

185. If you have ever sprayed on fake tan, then you are a woman. Put out an APB for your testicles, bitch.

186. When answering the question about how long sex was, feel free to add about twenty minutes. All that lying you did to get her into bed has to count for something.

187. If you ever get a call girl or stripper, pay her in one of those big empty water jugs full of change: $250 worth of change is heavy as shit, and well worth watching her struggle it into an elevator then subsequent taxicab. Obviously refrain from doing this if her bodyguard is within one hundred yards.

188. After getting head from a girl with braces, make jokes about how you like riding the rails and henceforth refer to the girl as "Amtrak."

189. The next time you bone a chick, unaware of the fact she had a yeast infection until the deed was done, you have to say, "I was standing in the fucking bread-line and didn't even know it?!"

190. Women never forget anything. Whenever your girl brings up the time you cheated on her, say, "Oh yeah, that was some damn good sex." She will inevitably be pissed, but just remind her you had forgotten all about it until she brought it up. Watch her develop amnesia with amazing quickness.

191. A woman's self-esteem is like a roller coaster: the faster it drops, the more fun you have.

192. Men are stupid by nature; women choose to be stupid.

193. Buying a woman a diamond ring is like putting the silencer on a gun and then shooting yourself with it.

194. The only bust in your house should be the huge one on your girl's chest.

195. Being late to an event of your own accord is fine, but being late because of a woman is inexcusable. Next time, just leave her. This is why they invented cell phones and MapQuest. She'll be mad, but hopefully by the time she arrives, you'll be too drunk to care.

196. Immediately Rolodex any girl that doesn't give head under "Betamax." Feel free to call her this in public

so as to let the others know she is an outdated model.

197. When a chick says she doesn't give head, lovingly hold her and tell her it's okay and it's not a problem . . . because other girls will.

198. As satisfying as that *thwap* sound is, refrain from slapping your meat across a girl's ass. Her forehead is a much more fulfilling target.

199. Women get mad for long periods of time over the dumbest shit. This is unavoidable. So just ignore the problem until she or the problem goes away. If she stays, eventually this is called marriage.

200. After asking your woman for the 875th time, "What's the matter?" without getting a response, you are entitled to dash her head on the fireplace. Just kidding, that would stain the carpet.

201. Telling a woman to "get over it," is just like trying to park a semi in your living room. That shit will never happen.

202. If you lie to her, you get yelled at. If you tell the truth, you get yelled at. The lesson here is to never speak to a woman unless you need something. Anything else will get you in trouble. It is a sad, sad truth.

203. Listening to a woman drone on and on about her day is way easier if you are mentally (or actually) undressing her.

204. When referring to your girlfriend or wife around your buddies, it is always fun to refer to her as your "cock-mitten." Unless of course your "girlfriend" or "wife" is an actual mitten that you masturbate with, in which case you need to invest $100 for a decent-looking hooker. (The one without too many track marks on her arm or a crack pipe in her pocket.)

205. If she's too big to pick up and bang against a wall, then you probably shouldn't take her home . . . unless you are wasted or slump busting. In that case, give that large lass all she can handle. Just make sure she's there and gone before the end of the late-night Cinemax movie.

206. When you were growing up, did you ever wonder which of your buddies' moms gave the best blow jobs? Neither did we, so don't talk about it . . . even though you still know exactly who it would be.

207. When a man gets home from work, all he wants is to drink a beer, watch the game, and get a blow job. When your woman gets home, she wants to talk on and on about her day. Try grabbing a beer, turning on the game, and putting your cock in her mouth while she talks. This way, everyone wins.

208. Some girls like to hook up with guys at random, don't care about exchanging phone numbers, and claim that they're not interested in a relationship. Never hook up with a girl like this in the dark . . . If you must turn off the lights, check thoroughly for the remnants of a penis before beginning.

209. Before you get married, think hard on this question: Which is better, waking up in the arms of a woman you know, love, and trust, or waking up with the blankets missing, the sheets up your ass crack, and a hot naked woman next to you whose face you don't recognize, lying in a slick of mixed reproductive juices?

210. Do not try to convert a wild slut into a tame wife. This is like trying to walk a hyena with a leash.

211. If your wife found out what happened at your bachelor party and wasn't shocked into seriously reconsidering the marriage, then one or both of the following are true:

    • Your wife is a dirty slut and you should find a new one.
    • Your bachelor party was really lame and you don't deserve happiness.

212. If you are lucky enough to have sex in the morning before work, make it a point not to wash your hands, and then shake the hand of every person you see that day. If you masturbate in the morning before work . . .

well, that's just sad. In fact, you probably don't have a job. Or you're a lawyer.

213. If you're really desperate to meet chicks, ride the subway with a copy of Shakespeare's plays. Open it and stare blankly at the pages. We guarantee you'll get hit on.

214. If a girl has a more manly tattoo than you would ever get, do not have sex with her. We promise, she's going to want to fuck you with a double-headed dildo.

215. Goth chicks are scary. If you ever make out with one, make sure you aren't that drunk. There's nothing worse than lying on your back watching some crazy bitch who literally looks like a witch cackle with delight while she spins above you.

216. Given how much men hate to be ordered around by their women, it is a real moral quandary when a woman orders you to do something you already wanted to do. On that note, *Man: The Book* says that if a woman ever orders you to drink beer, watch porn, or play golf, you are permitted to follow this order without being considered whipped.

217. Being "whipped" by your woman is one thing; actually having your woman administer a leather whip in the bedroom is quite another. In either case, this is not something you want to tell your friends about.

218. If your wife or girlfriend owns a dildo and uses it on you, it's just courtesy to wash it off afterward.

219. No matter who you are, unless you are rich or famous, the following women (if at least mildly attractive) are too hot and cool for you, and can only be admired from afar. Any attempt to seduce them will only end in heartbreak:

     • Bartenders
     • Aerobics/dance/yoga instructors
     • Strippers
     • NCAA Division athletes in the following sports: soccer, lacrosse, field hockey

220. If you are forced to go shopping for drapes with your woman, insist on getting black drapes. When asked why, say it's because you want them to be opaque so "there will be no witnesses."

221. Alternatively, exclaim loudly that you would like "shaved" drapes, to ensure that "your carpet matches your curtains." High-five the nearest man.

222. Being at a sporting event or being too drunk are perfectly valid reasons for missing a date with a girlfriend.

223. If you ever find yourself folding your girl's laundry for her, you're probably missing a testicle—you should get that checked out.

224. It is okay in any setting to point out, apropos of nothing, that men are better drivers than women are.

225. A man never relinquishes control of the radio to a woman. Never.

226. If your wife or girlfriend ever makes you see a "chick flick," you should make her give you a blow job that night to balance things out. If you see a chick flick with any woman who is not a wife or girlfriend, you should kick yourself in the face for being a pussy.

227. If you first see her in a bathing suit at a water park with her family, she is too young . . . so you probably don't need a condom.

228. Under no circumstances may any man describe a fat woman using the phrase "Her face is really cute."

229. A man may not laugh at the jokes of a girl in the presence of other men unless they are actually funny. This means he will only ever laugh at what a girl says in the presence of Sarah Silverman and Tina Fey.

230. If your girlfriend dumps you, immediately make out with someone she knows and make certain she knows about it.

231. The best way to attract a woman is to wear a wedding ring. If you don't have a wedding ring, try covering your body in $100 bills . . . women are shallow.

232. Kissing, holding hands, and all other forms of affection should not be shown in public unless *both* the following are true:

    • She is your wife / girlfriend.
    • She is so extraordinarily hot that she will make all other men within a quarter-mile radius envy you.

233. Remember, girls are for keeping, ho's are for sharing. Don't be rude.

234. Tell a girl you know the location of Atlantis, the Honeycomb Hideout, and Mayberry. If she believes two out of three, she is 66 percent pure dumb-ass. She is ripe for the picking.

235. If you ever see an incredibly attractive woman sitting by herself in a Vegas casino, assume she is either a prostitute or she just got off work. Either way, you should attempt to hit on her because, no matter which of the two she is, you have a good chance of getting laid.

236. "What happens in Vegas stays in Vegas . . . ," so go ahead and let that candy-hiding tranny prostitute bang you until your ass bleeds. Wait . . .

237. Jerking off to a kid's television show is only acceptable if the host is so hot she even makes third graders hard, you pause the DVR frame for self-pleasure, and no kids are visible.

238. Any woman you sleep with must be more than half and less than twice your age.

239. If you met her in a bar and bedded her, for God's sake, don't marry her. She is clearly a slut.

240. The number of minutes you spend talking to a fat or ugly girl in a bar must be less than the number of hot friends she has with her.

241. If you cheat on your girlfriend with someone she knows, you have no one to blame but yourself when she tells on you.

242. Feel free to lie liberally about how often you and your girlfriend have sex and how many orgasms she has; never lie about how much you bench.

243. It is a must to attempt any and all sexual positions with an animal name in it, e.g., the flying squirrel, doggy style, the sidewinder, and the horse-and-buggy. Addendum: All moves with WWE names such as the pile driver and the figure four are only to be done with drunken harlots who shall be released back into the wild the next day. This is called "catch-and-release."

244. If you wake up next to a woman who is not your wife, and you hear a child crying in the next room, get out fast and don't go back. If you forget anything in her house, it's hers.

245. To find out if a girl is a slut, the next time you get a blow job, make the Tim "Tool Man" Taylor Tool Time man-grunt during the opening stanza. If she finishes, you have your answer. Proceed with caution.

246. If a woman asks you to give up your dog, respond nonverbally by murdering her cat in front of her and feeding the carcass to your dog. When he starts eating, turn back to your woman and say, simply, "No."

247. Be very careful about hastily presuming a girl is "locked down." You never know when Chris Berman might walk into the bar and take your girl away.

248. No woman has ever looked good in a one-piece bathing suit in your eyes . . . ever.

249. If you own action figures still in their original plastic cases and a girl is willing to have sex with you, marry her now before she realizes she is sleeping with a guy who keeps action figures in their original plastic cases.

250. The general rule with hot white-trash women: look but don't touch.

251. If a girl will blow you while you watch a football game, you should marry her.

252. Whenever possible, categorize females by using some system other than their names. This will allow you

to freely immerse yourself into a flock of hot females and discuss their hotness right among them, without being discovered. To illustrate, the hot girl who sometimes wears a pink headband to the gym while riding the elliptical machine, can be referred to as "Pink Headband Girl," even if she later does not wear the pink headband. As you and your friends become more proficient with this technique, shorter names, or even acronyms, may be employed. For instance, "Pink Headband Girl" may be shortened to "PHG." Other examples include initially referring to the female you met at church as, "Church Girl," and later as, "Jesus." If rushed, and there is no time to properly coin such a pseudonym, refer to a hot woman simply as "Hal." For example, imagine a hot girl walking up to two unsuspecting men. To confirm hotness, Man #1 at some point in the conversation should ask Man #2, "By the way, is Hal here?" If the female is, in fact, hot, Man #2 should reply with something along the lines of, "Oh yes, Hal has been here all night."

253. If a woman suggests you should consider giving up sugary cereals, break up with her. If you are already married, this is sufficient grounds for divorce.

254. As bare breasts are the reward, all men must be able to unhook any type of bra in under thirty seconds. Flip the girl over if necessary. Just don't go past thirty seconds.

255. Pissing on a girl during a freaky-ass night of sexy isn't nasty, seeing her again is.

256. When relating a hookup story to your friends, chest size is much more important than her name.

257. A man keeps track of the similarities between himself and Brad Pitt (besides the possible latent homosexuality) and is able to use them as confidence boosters before hitting on a woman.

258. If you remember nothing else from this book, make this phrase your credo: All women are sluts, some just don't know it yet.

259. If you had sex with a transsexual while she was a female you are still gay, because you had sex with a man. Feel doubly worse because you might be the one that turned her. If your friends don't know, feel like the luckiest gay man alive.

260. Once she is past eighteen, you are never, ever, "doing her first." Come on, man. She's fucking lying to you.

261. When you move in together with your girlfriend, make sure she understands the most important bathroom/bedroom rules: If it's brown, flush it down; if it's white, drink it down.

262. Next time a woman utters the phrase, "There are no good guys left out there," feel free to respond, "Did you ever consider the opposite?" If she argues with you, eventually agree with her position and introduce

her to the worst guy you know with a glowing rec-
ommendation.

263. There are probably tons of reasons why you thought
blowing a kiss to your significant other was okay.
Unfortunately for you, every one of them was wrong.

264. If you *ever* are lucky enough to "make love" to a female bartender or a stripper, then they really like you.
Seriously. Whatever you said or did to get them into
bed was obviously quite awesome. Keep it to yourself. Consider yourself a God amongst men. You may
ignore one man rule per every freaky sexual dalliance.

265. Women like funny, honest men. The next time you drive
by a girl making "The Walk of Shame" the next morning, yell out the window, "He couldn't even give you cab
money!! And you slept with him?!" If you see this girl
later, divulge to her this irony and attempt to sleep with
her with a clear conscience. Then don't give her cab
money the next morning. This is the Circle of Slut Life.

266. If your girl wears the same thong for two days straight,
she should not be your girl anymore. She is a skankbot.

267. Beware of a woman who claims she only wants sex
and not a relationship. This is a lie. She is like a hungry fox hiding in the bushes waiting to pounce on
your testicles at the first sign of weakness.

268. Getting into a car accident while staring at a hot girl
is a good excuse to hit on her, unless she was actu-

ally harmed in the accident, in which case you probably shouldn't hit on her.

269. Blue balls really do exist. If a girl gives you blue balls,
feel free to finish yourself off and leave the evidence
in her sock drawer.

270. If a girl's mother looks like she just survived a grenade
assault, run in the opposite direction.

271. A man enters a grocery store only to purchase Gatorade
and pick up milfs. There is a pun here with the "milk
aisle" and the "milf aisle" but we're not seeing it.

272. If your buddy responds, "I don't kiss and tell," when
asked about the details of a hookup, then he did not
get any and probably never will with any woman.

273. Whenever you are caught checking out another woman,
turn to your girlfriend or wife, act as if you had just
been in an emotional trance, and say "I love you."

274. The number of times in one day that you say the words
"I love you," to the woman you are with must be less
than the number of times you said, "That girl's hot,"
to one of your male friends when seeing another girl.

275. If you see an ugly guy with a hot girl on his arm,
give him a nod. That man is rich; he just might tip
you.

276. When in a meeting, if you find yourself doodling on a pad of paper, just make sure the naked woman you're drawing doesn't look like your boss or co-worker.

277. If you suddenly realize as she approaches that a girl you have been checking out from a distance is not attractive, change your look to one of scorn and make it clear that she is not worthy to walk the same street as you.

278. You are never too old to enjoy a wet T-shirt contest. Unless your daughter is involved; then you are too old.

279. If a girl shows you her tattoo, then she will have sex with you. This means that girls with openly visible tattoos will have sex with anyone.

280. As a general rule, any vacation that requires women to put more clothes on when you arrive at your destination than women were wearing when you left is not really a vacation.

281. If a woman talks dirty during sex, you are strongly encouraged to audio-record it and play it for your friends.

282. When shopping with a woman, the response to the inevitable, "Will you hold my purse for me while I try this on?" is, "Will you blow me in the dressing room?" Alternatively, the man may not respond at all

because he has departed long ago for Sports Authority or the cigar store.

283. Looking for nipples in movies is never a boring pastime. Feel free to pause, edit, change the screen color, or buy a new wider-screen television. Basically, feel free to do whatever you need to do to be able to see an artfully disguised nipple.

284. If a hot mother is breast-feeding her child, you may discreetly check out her boobs.

285. There have never been heels that were too high or skirts that were too short. Shaw dissents here: "What if a woman's heels were five feet tall? Then they would clearly be too high."

286. Each man may have one woman whom he considers to be so attractive he would allow her to screw him with a dildo in exchange for sex. Admittedly, this is controversial.

287. You may be troubled by society's objectification of women only when being troubled by society's objectification of women helps you get laid.

288. *Premarital Piss*: This is the infuriating state of affairs that men dwell in as the wedding approaches. It is located polar opposite from Premarital Bliss, which is what women experience. Bitterness, scorn, and short-tempered calls and e-mails to your peers, especially

single ones, are not uncommon. Moments of rage bordered by fits of blindness are also common side effects. It's hard to be happy, particularly when your nuts have been handcuffed to your asshole and you have to pick out bouquet arrangements, taste wedding cakes, and attempt to stave off attacks from your buddies about why you are acting so strangely.

289. If a girl can take a shot of Rebel Yell or Old Crow like a champ, or enjoys watching porn with you, be wary. Immensely and immediately aroused, but wary.

290. If your friends ever learn that you have turned down a blow-job offer from a woman at anytime in your life, they are allowed to take turns ritualistically kicking you in your shins and punching you in the throat. A blow-job offer should never be turned down . . . ever. . . . We can't stress this enough.

291. It is excusable if you get wasted one night and end up having wild sex with a random unhot, fat, old, or skanky woman due to the fact that you were not coherent and your decision skills were hampered. Banging her again the next morning is not only inexcusable but deplorable.

292. If you get caught grabbing a female's ass while out with friends and she turns and comes back to you with a vile, hate-filled glare in her eyes, simply say, "I'm sorry, I thought you were my sister." This will

repulse her or make her laugh. Either way, you are no worse off.

293. Never hook up with a girl if you're not strong enough to pick her up off the ground and lift her above your head.

294. If you meet a girl in a Halloween costume that consists of just a slutty outfit and a pair of bunny ears, make sure she wears them later that night when she rides you. It is acceptable to keep the ears as a souvenir when she leaves your apartment in the morning.

295. No more than one time per week, to make a point about how ugly a girl is, a man may utilize hyperbole and say he would rather sleep with a man. This is allowed unless it becomes a pattern, in which case the man is gay.

296. When frequenting or working at an establishment where there are a lot of girls employed, faithfully attempt to bed each one in succession. Don't worry if they find out or know about each other; try and collect the whole set. Watch them fight, and subsequently deplete the whole social order of the place of business and witness it rot away. This is called a "Staff Infection."

297. If your guy friend is out of town and you hang out with his girlfriend or wife alone, the lights must be on at all times. If you find out your buddy hung out with your woman in a dark room, you may murder him.

298. Even though it may seem like a good idea, hooking up with an Olympic gymnast is not recommended. They are mostly underage, have no breasts, and can probably bench-press you.

299. Play it safe: if you see a wedding ring on a woman's finger, make sure there are no huge guys in the vicinity before you go hit on her.

300. If a friend of yours hooks up in your old college dorm after five or more years, you owe him a night of drinks. If he hooks up with your younger sister in your old college dorm, you owe him a fist.

301. When a girl who is not your wife or longtime girlfriend sends you a *Penthouse* forum–type e-mail or naked pictures, it is mandatory to show them to every male friend you have known for longer than thirteen months.

302. Hitting on a woman who is with her kids is acceptable in only two situations.

    (1) She ranks higher than 9 on the hotness scale, or

    (2) You are incredibly intoxicated.

303. Obsessively following around a hot girl at the gym or the mall is not psycho. Well, yes it is, but don't let that stop you.

304. Age of consent is only an issue if you actually have sex. Looking is no crime.

305. If you see a girl out in public wearing clear high heels, feel free to approach and offer her a dollar to see her boobs.

306. Female co-workers are to be treated with respect. Say "nice ass," instead of just slapping it.

307. Unfortunately, driver education has misinformed so much of the population—the rearview mirror is for checking out girls walking behind the car. That's why it rotates.

308. Sleeping with the old high school teacher you once had a crush on is fully sanctioned. If she has aged beyond recognition, her hotness is still registered at her former level.

309. If she cheats on you and videotapes it, you have a duty to secure a copy of the tape and tearfully masturbate to it.

310. Remember that anal sex with a woman is, anatomically, basically the same as anal sex with a man.

311. Never, ever, play strip poker without a camera present. If a girl tells you not to take pictures, she isn't drunk enough yet. She'll get there.

312. Every man should have a friend that he can blame for any sort of trouble that he gets into. This friend shall be called the "parachute friend" and your wife or girlfriend will absolutely hate this friend. For example,

if a spouse finds a bra that is not hers, you can blame it on the parachute friend saying he was at the house over the weekend and took some random skank home. You should take the parachute friend to at least three sporting events per year, paying for all his food and drinks, as payment for the unjustified wrath he has suffered from your wife or girlfriend.

313. If you play a game of strip poker and no woman ends up naked at the end, you have squandered an opportunity and are never allowed to play again. Also, you need to learn how to cheat better.

314. Five-hundred-dollar-a-night hookers make much more sense if you itemize the money you spend on dates.

315. A man may always loan his coat or jacket to a cold woman, but he may never borrow a woman's jacket when he is cold.

316. On demand, every man must be able to admit the female cartoon character he would choose to have sex with.

317. No matter what, if you are already having sex before marriage, you will never have more sex after marriage. Disregard at your own peril.

318. We've all been fed a horrible lie. Women do not want to have sex anywhere near as much as men. Period. Accepting this may make you cry for a month. This is okay, it's better that you know it now.

III.

Manican't

MITCH MARTIN: *Sorry, your seatbelt seems to be broken. What do you recommend I do?*
CAB DRIVER: *I recommend you stop being such a faggot. You're in the backseat.*
—Old School

We can spot a tool from a mile away. Trust us, we can. His gel is sparkling, his wristbands are vintage, and sometimes he forgets to take off his Crest Whitestrips before he goes out to the bar. When it's cold, he insists on wearing a scarf, and when he drinks alcohol at a bar, there is always a pink hue to his drink. He knows what color saffron is and he matches his shoelaces to his belt. He never laughs, he always giggles, and there has never been a time when he uses the word *homie* without irony. This is a subtle change from ten years ago when he constantly referred to everyone as *homes-skillet*.

He wears cologne and pays more than twenty dollars for a haircut. If he is balding, he pays thousands of dollars a year for hair-plugs and hides his Rogaine pills behind his Viagra pills. He dances along to the most current songs even though he doesn't know any words other than the chorus, which he insists on singing at the top of his voice while pointing at you.

He has silk sheets even though he has to constantly replace them because he has wet dreams every time he rolls over in bed and thinks he is touching a girl's panties. The girls he dates will all have bags under their eyes and asses like saddles. They will all have been ridden for a very long time and their voices will sound like sandpaper being scraped over a blackboard.

He will have no body hair except for a soul patch or sideburns or a mustache so thin it resembles a skimming layer of chocolate milk. He will incorrectly use words that he hears from rap songs and, if he wears a T-shirt, he will make sure he also wears his fake Rolex. If he is wealthy enough to afford a real Rolex and he wears a T-shirt, he will make frequent reference to the time and say things like, "Lemme check the Rollie." He will shorten all words, even words that do not need shortening, and his girlfriend's hair will never be its original color. He will be very fond of the fist-bump and you will always want to punch him with your own fist in the temple.

He will never have said anything funny in his life but he will always lead the group in laughter. If something funny is actually said, he will not laugh. He will wear boxer briefs and flex his puny arms in the mirror while he sprays fake-tan oils on his pale body. He will constantly assert that he "got the hookup" even though, at no point, will he ever hook you up with anything. He will constantly get in fake bar fights with other poodle men of his own ilk until one day when he bumps into an actual man and says, "Watch it, homes," and the actual man will pull back his fist and pummel him to within an inch of his life. You will be there, watching and rooting for him to be lifted up and impaled on the Jagermeister shot machine. Later, he will speak to you with a gauze pad attached to his swollen tongue. "Why didn't you step in, homes-skillet?" he will ask. Hopefully, by that point you will pass him a copy of this book and say, "Because, like everyone else, I was hoping you would die."

319. If your girlfriend bakes cookies without sugar because she wants you to eat healthier, throw yourself off the balcony. If you do not have a balcony, a staircase will do. If you have neither a balcony nor a staircase, you are living in a trailer park and nothing can save you.

320. If you're tweezing your eyebrows, you might as well go ahead and wax your labia, too.

321. Never flick off truckers. Seriously. Think about it. You drive all day in a semi and some punk kid comes along and flicks you off. Most people would let this go. But if we were driving a truck, we would try and kill you.

322. When cutting down trees never call out, "Timber!" to another man you are working with. If his stupid ass can't tell that a tree is about to fall, he deserves to be pinned beneath it.

323. After he sprouts pubic hair, no man may engage in a "Who can blow the biggest chewing gum bubble" contest with any other man. If you see this happening, feel free to assume both men are comfortable with sticky faces.

324. Everyone has seen that video where the woman sucks the horse's cock until the horse comes all over her face. Not everyone has masturbated to it. You sick fuck.

325. Riding a watery amusement park ride and attempt-

ing to avoid getting wet is like going to a strip club and cringing every time a breast comes near you. Don't be a pussy. Root for the water . . . and the tits.

326. Don't ever go swimming in the ocean with a woman who is on her period.

327. Playing thumps or slaps is the only time your hand should ever touch another man's hand outside of a sporting event.

328. If you can't keep a canoe going straight in the center of the river, focus on tipping other people over. If you can't tip anyone over, either, don't go on a damn canoe trip.

329. Once he is out of high school, a man may never describe his sexual activity utilizing the baseball/bases metaphor. No one cares about your hot make-out session and the fact that you brushed a girl's breast. Unless you're Mormon. Then, by all means, share your make-out story and breast rubbing, so long as you are aware that, later, the other guys will be thinking of you when they have wet dreams in their Mormon underpants.

330. By all means, shave your pubic hair. You want him to be able to find your asshole, don't you?

331. No man may put an orange wedge into his beer. Just drink your damn beer. This also goes for limes in Coronas unless you are legitimately at the beach. If you're

at a crowded bar and you request limes for your Corona, the bartender can have you held down while he squirts lime juice into your eyes and beats you with his drink mixer.

332. *Not* attempting to discreetly look up a girl's skirt while she rides up the escalator is actually the offensive thing to do. Trust us.

333. The next time your buddy tells you a story about the gang bang he watched on tape, please resist asking this question, "Was she hot?" Yes, we're sure she was the hottest girl on the face of the earth. She had the best qualities of Eva Longoria, Vanessa Millo, and Jessica Simpson combined. No, you fuck-face, she was a grotesque ugly whore with a vagina so big you could climb inside her and use her clitoris for a boxing bag.

334. If at any point your friend ever uses the phrase, "Don't hate the player, hate the game," while he's talking on the phone to his girlfriend who already has two children under five, you are permitted to drown him in a toilet.

335. At any time, if a dude in a sweater vest aces you out for a girl, you have to walk outside and lay your body down in the center of a busy street *Program*-style. If the dude in the sweater vest subsequently comes outside and tries to get you to climb out of the street, you have to stand and throw yourself at an oncoming car.

336. No man interacts with mascots at sporting events. Trust us, the guy who gets up and does high-kicks on top of the dugout with the San Diego Chicken is going to be choking his own chicken.

337. Unless he lives in Sudan, a man can't complain about not getting to eat on time. Chill out, you pussy. Eventually, we promise, you will eat again. You're not going to starve.

338. You were NEVER a virgin.

339. Never "sidle" or "pony" up to the bar. Sit the fuck down and have a drink.

340. Unless they add a nudity competition, watching any beauty pageant is strictly forbidden. Okay, you can keep watching Cocksucker 48, too.

341. The only dog competition you have ever seen had better have been at a track, or in a shed out in Tijuana that ends in gruesome death.

342. The ability to "take one on the chin" is fine, unless they are talking about dicks . . . or balls.

343. The only stained glass in your house should be your bongs.

344. Limit one tablecloth per table. They get in the way of table sex, and of course there's the temptation to do that dumbass trick where you break all the dishes.

345. Cooking shows are strictly forbidden. If you can't operate a microwave, Foreman grill, or light some charcoal, you deserve to die the slow death starvation brings.

346. Anytime you get the chance to pick your jersey number, never pick 00, 0, or 1. This makes you look like an attention-seeking twat. Donning number 69 has the same effect and guarantees that people will make jokes about your being part of an all-man seesaw.

347. Depending on the quality of the money shot, a porn may only be dubbed over by a classic playoff game or that clip of those crocs mowing down those wildebeests crossing a river in Africa.

348. Pissing on yourself while drunk is pretty foul but acceptable drunken behavior. Shitting on yourself is sick and deplorable. But what's worse is when you put your hands down there and then smell them—like your nasty ass didn't know it was shit.

349. Unless they have mauling tendencies, a man should never own two dogs that look exactly the same. And, under no circumstances, can a man own two dogs and name them something like Thelma and Louise.

350. There is a saying (actually it's a country song): "the clothes don't make the man" . . . which directly contradicts Shakespeare's quote to the contrary. Listen to Wild Bill: take off that yellow mesh football jersey and put on a T-shirt. That is, of course, unless you are, or want people to think you are, gay or European.

351. When at the swimming pool over the summer, re-member this: No man ever looks cool diving. Even if you're good at it, it still looks pretty fruity. So do every other guy there a favor and do a cannonball, making sure to splash the girls lying out in the white bikinis.

352. If the guy who is winning in your fantasy sports pool is also the same guy who doesn't keep his team up-dated, resist the urge to murder him with your bare hands. Your reward is waiting in heaven.

353. Having a favorite Golden Girl is absolutely *not* cool. But, obviously, it's Blanche.

354. If you ever accidentally watch *What Women Want*, starring Mel Gibson, your missing testicles can be found underneath a copy of *Mad Max*.

355. Regardless of what you tell your woman while she's away, never tell another man that you "miss her so much," unless you are referring specifically to forni-cation.

356. If anyone makes a suggestion as to how the game of basketball could be better by referencing MTV's Rock and Jock challenge, feel free to never listen to any-thing he ever says again.

357. No plate less than twenty-five pounds may be uti-lized in the weight room at any time. Ten- and five-pound plates may be used only as weapons.

358. If you know the names of more than two members

of any boy band, pierce through your eardrums with a smoldering sharpened pike. This will prevent you from ever listening to music again.

359. Puffy gloves may not be worn by any man. If you don't know whether your gloves are puffy or not, trust us, they're too puffy.

360. One man shall never utter the phrase "boo-yah" for any other reason other than mocking Stuart Scott.

361. A man (call him Man 1) may refer to another man (Man 2) as *brosef*, but must then immediately challenge him to a fight. If Man 1 loses the fight, he must then commit ritualistic samurai suicide with a plastic dinner knife. If Man 1 wins the fight, he may call the other man *brosef*. At any point in the future, Man 2 may then call a challenge to the outcome of the fight. If Man 1 turns down the challenge, he must cease calling Man 2 *brosef*. This cannot be reversed. If Man 1 accepts the challenge and wins, he may kill Man 2 with his bare hands. If Man 1 accepts but then loses, he becomes *brosef*. This process may continue back and forth until one of the men dies. The man who remains living must then deliver the eulogy at the dead man's funeral, referring to him only as *brosef* in his speech. He then assumes control of all of *brosef*'s possessions, including his girlfriend or wife, who must submit to him completely.[*]

---

[*]Hopefully, reading this long and unfunny rule has convinced you of the ridiculousness of ever using the word *brosef*

362. No Halloween costume for any man can be remotely sexy; by contrast, every woman's costume must be slutty.

363. If you do not know the definition of the following terms, fake it, and keep your mouth closed, missy: *icing*, *illegal defense*, *offsides*, *birdie*, and *West Coast offense*.

364. Since 1997 is over, no more tribal band tattoos allowed. Period.

365. If one man buys a snow cone or cotton candy, no other man he is with may also buy a snow cone or cotton candy at the same time.

366. Voluntary plastic surgery is forbidden, unless medically required, or unless you are the surgeon. In that case, proceed and violate the Hippocratic Oath by posting before and after tit pics (without your patient's knowledge) on www.voyeur-web.com. Thanks.

367. If you have never been to a bachelor party or gone egging, go shave with a plastic disposable for a week. Each day, go play basketball. That'll learn you to not have cool friends. . . .

368. There are only three times a man can ask for help: when shopping for flowers, lingerie, or perfume. Any other time, we can figure it out on our own.

369. If you have a friend with an impressive physique, it is not okay to stare at him in awe as he does the bench press: there is no such thing as an appropriate non-sexual admiration of another man's muscles.

370. Just because you have a live studio audience laugh track in your head, doesn't mean you are actually funny.

371. Despite his newfound cult hero status, Chuck Norris's name is never to be mentioned, except in pure unadulterated jest.

372. No man may mention or inquire about another man's waist size. Ever.

373. If you are a single man and own a noncactus plant that lives longer than two months, check your pants for signs of vaginal residue. Plastic plants are the preferred style.

374. A man never answers any question with, "I don't know." A man never admits ignorance. If you don't know and can't make it up, the answer is, "I don't care."

375. A man does not own a cutting board, nor really knows what one is. He prepares all foods using a Bowie knife.

376. If a man owns more pairs of shoes than he does T-shirts, this means he is gay.

377. No man may wear camouflage unless he is actually attempting to kill something or playing paintball.

378. Under no circumstances can wine consumption ever be measured in glasses. Bottles, please.

379. Unless a legitimate sports star (All-American/Conference, 1st, 2nd, 3rd Teams, or Honorable Mention at the collegiate level; a professional NFL, MLB, or NBA player) or a rap artist, a man is entitled to wear no more than *three* pieces of jewelry at any given time. Acceptable jewelry includes a necklace with religious symbols, watches, bracelets, or earrings. Wedding rings are exempt. The foregoing rules pertain only to African-American men. Men of all other races, even if legitimate sports stars, are limited to *two* pieces of the aforementioned jewelry, not including earrings, which are forbidden, unless good cause is shown. "Good cause" is defined as "able to pull it off."

380. Never dance during any song by the Village People. If you catch yourself accidentally dancing to one of their songs, hustle to the nearest bar and order a glass of scotch immediately.

381. A man can never wear a helmet while riding a scooter. In fact, a man should never find himself seated upon a scooter unless he is on a small tropical island, or it is the only possible way for him to heroically rescue his equally heroic dog.

382. Men cannot use the "I was so drunk I didn't know what I was doing" line more than once a month. Any more times than once a month is disallowed for anyone but hot girls.

383. When in another man's car, you may not request a change of any kind to the climate control.

384. Everyone wanted to be Mr. T at some point in his life; this is okay to admit. However, not everyone wanted to be Daisy Duke. Keep both this and your vintage shorts to yourself.

385. A phone conversation between men can end at anytime by simply saying, "Gotta go, man," and hanging up. If a conversation between two men has lasted longer than three minutes, hang up immediately and start a fight with the closest man to you.

386. Man activities that cannot be mocked by another man: fishing, camping, contact sports, chewing tobacco, and drinking whiskey.

387. Never use the word *golly*.

388. No man will ever refer to sexual intercourse as *shagging*. Also, Austin Powers is *not* funny, but even less funny is your weak Austin Powers impersonation that always comes out after two beers. Do everyone a favor and stay home.

389. If a man ever wears a pink shirt, his friends are encouraged to have sex with his girlfriend. If a man ever wears pink pants, his friends are encouraged to have sex with his girlfriend or his sister. If a man ever wears both pink pants and a pink shirt at the same time, his friends are required to have sex with both his girlfriend and his sister.

390. Never allow mundane or awkward situations (e.g., long drive with just two males in the car) to force your hand into resorting to meaningful conversation with another man. That material is limited, so save it for people who care, like women. Some alternatives:

- The "Would You Rather" game: A classic question-and-answer session where one man asks the other to choose between two rather unenviable positions. For example, "Xang, would you rather eat a bowl of my back hair, or gently massage my inner thigh?" "Neither" is not an appropriate answer. Regardless of the answer, the interviewer must always reply with something like, "What?!?!?!? You're disgusting, man. You want to touch my thigh?!?!?"

- The "How Many Points Could I Score in An Entire NBA Season" quandary. The parameters of this hypothetical are: You are on an NBA team, and you play every minute of every game. You are on a middle-tier playoff team whose goal is to win a championship. How many total points would you score? If the respondent is someone of average height and athletic ability, answers above 15 total points per season should be met with ridicule. You can, of course, tweak this game to fit any of the major sports (how many yards would you rush for in an NFL season, how many goals would you score in an NHL season, how many hits in the MLB, what would you shoot at the Masters, etc).

391. A man never says the word *tipsy*.

392. No matter how much he wants his fifteen seconds of fame, a man never accepts an invitation to be on any show hosted by Carson Daly.

393. The bitch seat in the car may never be called. It is always assigned or relegated. If someone calls bitch, the driver may justifiably force that person to walk.

394. No matter how scary a movie is, two men may not sleep in the same room as a result thereof. And before you ask, that goes even if you live on Elm Street and Freddy Krueger was real.

395. If at any point in your life you have ever owned a lotion or grooming product with a name like Juniper Breeze, go ahead and use the Juniper Breeze to lube your asshole and wait for your fantasy to come true.

396. If another man asks you to throw something in the back of his truck, and when you go out to the truck

it is a Subaru Baja, this is not a man. It is most likely a homosexual man or bull dyke attempting to bed you. You should run over the Baja with your 3/4-ton pickup.

397. No silk shirts. Period.

398. A man may teach a woman to throw a football, but if a woman teaches you to throw a football, rip off your sac and give it to Ted Nugent. At least he'll know what to do with it.

399. Two men may not, under any circumstances, go shopping together.

400. Never wear a dress shirt with a collar that is a different color from the rest of the shirt.

401. If you see a black man with decorative scarification, do not mess with him but feel free to approach as normal. If you see a white man with scarification of any kind, this man is a psycho who might eat you and should be avoided at any cost.

402. A man may not apply bumper stickers to his car unless he also lives in said car with at least two hot women.

403. It's okay to admire another man who is very skilled at waterskiing, but it is also important to remember that said man is also very skilled at waterskiing. Don't overdo it.

404. If you are a man and you take ballet lessons, you are gay. Just accept this fact and move forward with your life.

405. Fame and fortune is no reason not to make fun of a friend's stupid haircut.

406. Only black men may wear jean shorts.

407. Never speak at the urinal to a man you don't know.

408. If a man does not know who Brutus the Barber Beefcake is, you cannot be friends with him.

409. At most, remember the year you met your buddy; anything more is unnecessary. Definitely no anniversaries.

410. Never threaten to slap another person, as in:
   - "I'm going to slap you"
   - "That kind of thing will get you slapped"

   Possible exception: a pimp may threaten to "pimp-slap" a woman, as in:
   - "Bitch, if you don't shut up, I'll pimp-slap you right across the face."

411. Unibrows are only sexy if you are the heavyweight champion of the world.

412. Male roommates may not have a Christmas tree unless it is undecorated. If tinsel is used or you are inclined to use tinsel, it means you are gay.

413. Nothing you have ever seen in your life has been cute. Ever.

414. Only turn on the air conditioner in your car when the temperature rises above ninety-eight degrees. At all other times, it's windows. Otherwise how are the women joggers going to hear you screaming, "Nice chimichangas."

415. If a man is wearing a sleeveless turtleneck, he should be pummeled to within an inch of his life.

416. Never fight a white-trash dude; you will get a disease.

417. Typing with two fingers is nothing to be ashamed of. Any man that disparagingly refers to this as "the hunt-and-peck method" in the presence of another man may, provided you are strong enough, have his nose used to replace your two fingers.

418. It doesn't matter how rich you are—never throw out your favorite T-shirt.

419. Always be familiar with the *TRO: Testicle Reappropriation Office*. This is where you have to go to get a little piece sliced off every time you hear that song with the words, "What if God was one of us?" Every

time they cut off a little slice, they give it to someone more deserving of their testicle matter, like Ted Nugent.

420. If a man has neither an Xbox nor a PlayStation, feel free to call his heterosexuality into question.

421. If a man does not know who Roscoe P. Coltrane was, you cannot be friends with him.

422. No man shall intentionally drive a Mazda Miata or VW Beetle in public.

423. If you find an empty wallet on the ground, you were too late.

424. A man may never exfoliate; in fact, a man should not even know what *exfoliate* means.

425. Knowing another man's suit measurements is way, way too much information. The most you should know is his T-shirt size.

426. Confiscate any Wu-Tang Clan stickers immediately. Any Wu-Tang tattoo discoveries deserve immediate and intense ridicule, unless it is actually one of the Wu-Tang Clan members. They will shoot you. Do not make fun of them.

427. Smiling while having your picture taken is not recommended. However, showing the camera your mid-

dle finger is both recommended and encouraged at all weddings. Women love that shit. Trust us.

428. Never refer to a Miata as "cool."

429. Calling the men's room "the little boy's room" is only funny if you are making a Michael Jackson joke. And then it's still not funny, you pedophile.

430. If another man ever says to you: "I don't even know who you are anymore," respond: "Still not gay," and never speak to this man again.

431. If a man denies ever having played Oregon Trail or Where in the World Is Carmen Sandiego? you cannot be friends with him.

432. A man may never go caroling.

433. If you utter the taunt, "Ref, get off your knees you're blowing the game," anyone within five rows of you in the arena has the right to lobotomize you with a plastic fork and knife.

434. A man may always taunt another man while playing SkeeBall, air hockey, or darts, but a man may never taunt another man while jumping rope.

435. Under no circumstances may a man partake in hot yoga.

436. If you visit an adult bookstore and ask if they have a particular DVD in stock, you are a pervert. Period. There are fourteen million porn DVDs to choose from and you know enough to ask for specific ones? But, obviously, you were asking for *College Invasion VI*, right?

437. Whenever another man says to you, "I just really don't care how big my television is," there is a 100 percent chance he sings along to musical soundtracks.

438. Remember how in first grade everybody gave butterfly kisses that consisted of rubbing your eyelashes against somebody else's skin while giggling? Wait . . . we don't remember that, either. If, perchance, you ever see a grown man doing this thing that none of us remember, please shoot him in the eyes with a nail gun.

439. Under no circumstances does the driver's girlfriend get automatic shotgun. If she calls it, fine, but there is nothing wrong with her sitting bitch in the backseat.

440. Even if it is the perfect size, a man may not use a pink or lavender bowling ball.

441. Never get a haircut that takes longer than fourteen minutes to complete or involves a hairdresser with less than a C-cup. Admit it, you enjoy when her breasts touch you.

442. Do not go to a postsunset movie showing with an-
     other man unless *all* of the following are true:

     (1) The movie involves nudity and/or greater than
         eight killings.

     (2) At least one empty seat is left between you.

     (3) The movie is rated R.

443. Unless it is a caged wild tiger of some kind, you may
     never own a cat. This especially applies to single men.
     There is a reason dogs are called man's best friend.
     If you are single with a cat, you need to take a good
     long look at your nether region and decide if it's
     worth keeping.

444. However, if you absolutely must own a cat, dress it
     in a football helmet as much as possible, 'cause that's
     rad.

445. If you are wearing tights, you had better be a super-
     hero.

446. Never admit that any animated film was funny, en-
     tertaining, or clever. If the animated film was funny,
     entertaining, or clever, a simple "It was decent. Just
     not my thing" will suffice. (McCrary notes: "I once
     admitted that *Shrek 2* was good, and immediately felt
     my right testicle shrink like a dried plum. I had to
     watch some lesbian porn to regain all function down
     there.")

447. White slacks may never be worn. The only exception is if you are a Cuban druglord, in which case your automatic weapon evens things out. Conversely, girls should wear white pants daily.

448. If you are older than three and you own some sort of stuffed animal, then go ahead and admit that you have a crush on A. C. Slater.

449. A man may use toothpaste and floss to care for his teeth but may never use Crest Whitestrips unless his teeth are darker brown than the lightest-colored Arizona Wildcats basketball player.

450. Never purchase a dog that, at full growth, is smaller than the distance between your elbow and the tip of your index finger.

451. A man may never go swimming wearing a T-shirt. If you have man-boobs, you aren't fooling anyone.

452. When eating popcorn, no two men may share a bucket, bowl, or any other device that may necessitate touching of oily fingers.

453. A man's shower may not take longer than five minutes. Any man that spends more than five minutes in a shower may be publicly accused, tried, and convicted, of shower masturbation. Preferably, this trial will take place in front of his girl.

454. Baseball caps may be worn forward or backward, but never sideways. If you see anyone you are bigger than wearing his hat sideways, be sure and notify him, his hat is not on straight.

455. If you are naked in the locker room and you have a towel wrapped around your shoulders but not wrapped around your waist, something is very wrong. Ask Andy Dufresne.

456. A man may never challenge another man to a pool handstand contest.

457. Under no circumstances may you use :) (or any other emoticon) when typing an email.

458. No call placed after 2:00 A.M. should be to another male unless it's to bail you out of jail. :-(

459. The following colors do not exist in a man's vocabulary; periwinkle, chartreuse, seacrest green, purple. In fact, any color can be described in one of the following ways: *cool* or *pussy*.

460. If you send a postcard to a man while you are in a foreign country, upon your return he can use said postcard to give you paper cuts on each of your fingers. This will teach you a lesson you should have already known . . . men don't write postcards to other men.

461. No matter how aggressive the prompting, you do not remember the words to either "Rudolph the Red Nosed Reindeer" or "Frosty the Snowman."

462. Everyone has a friend who has read one book in his life and will make analogies to every situation that ever occurs in his life based on this one book. There is a 90 percent chance that book will be *Lord of the Flies*. Feel free to penalize him by instituting a ten beers for every LOF analogy.

463. Riding in a limo if you aren't actually rich is really, really lame. Who are you fooling when you roll up at dollar beer night? It's like prom night except back then you didn't have acne or genital warts.

464. A man is allowed one nonsexual crush at a time on another man he does not know. He is allowed no nonsexual crushes on any man he actually knows.

465. Never hire movers. If you and two buddies can't move a piece of furniture by yourselves, a pox on you and yours.

466. Any pants that frame your cock are disallowed unless there is a signature dildo that bears your name.

467. A man keeps two stacks of porn: one (usually straight-forward guy + girl) that he doesn't mind sharing with friends, and the freaky one he actually likes. Under no condition should you willingly admit to the sec-

ond collection, nor should you risk showing it to your friends.

468. When watching a horror movie, never show any signs of fear. If you begin to feel the unfamiliar twinge of terror overcoming you, comment on the size of the breasts of one of the actresses.

469. A man may not have only a mustache unless he is starring in a remake of *Magnum P.I.*

470. Blue or black ink, please. Leave the light purple and sea green pens for third grade girls who dot their *i*'s with heart shapes. Do not dot your *i*'s with a heart shape, or any other shape for that matter, besides the classic dot.

471. You may never use phrases such as LOL, BFF, or any other acronyms that deserve to get you slapped.

472. Nothing has occurred since fourth grade that justifies either skipping or humming along to the song "Skip to My Lou My Darling." In fact, we apologize for remembering this song. Just don't skip.

473. After he passes the age when the practice is not required in school lines or music class, a man shall only hold hands with another man:

   • At his mother's funeral just after his sobbing father has asked for his hand; or
   • If he is gay.

474. Never do today what is due tomorrow. Then, call in sick tomorrow.

475. No man may surrender without being shot in paint-ball. If he does, every person playing paintball gets the opportunity to shoot him while he stands covering his genitals like a soccer penalty kick is about to be taken.

476. Do not be that guy who waits idly in one row of a crowded parking lot for a spot to open. Instead, drive around said parking lot with squinted eyes, like the territorial hunter that you are, and steal the spot from that guy. You may also pretend that you are a shark, patrolling your subterranean lair.

477. A man shall never purchase an ice-cream cone, lest he be mistaken for a tranny trying to make a little side cash. If a man must consume ice cream in public, then he may only do so at a ball game out of a miniature baseball helmet.

478. No straight man may wear a scarf . . . ever. If your neck is truly cold, wrap yourself in your boyfriend's tender embrace.

479. Ordering diet or lowfat anything under the age of thirty-two will get you beat down. Put down the pudding cup, lard-ass, and work out. Diabetics excluded, of course.

480. If Frank the Tank did not teach you at least five life lessons, then put down this book, walk out of the store, and reassess your life's priorities.

481. Never drive below the posted speed limit. Any car that passes you should be seen as a challenge and threat, and you should use all necessary means to overtake them.

482. If you believe earrings are appropriate if done tastefully, you are correct. Put them on your vagina. You are a girl.

483. Two men walking down an empty hallway may not acknowledge each other except by glaring or scowling. Smiling is absolutely forbidden. Black men are completely exempt from this rule.

484. If you are white, do not wear articles of clothing with the Confederate flag; if you are black, do not wear Malcolm X T-shirts. Conversely, if you are black, feel free to wear articles of clothing with the Confederate flag, and if you are white, feel free to wear Malcolm X T-shirts. If you are Asian or mixed, this becomes more complicated.

485. Under no circumstances can two men share a seat on a roller coaster when one man has to sit in between the other man's legs.

486. Drunk walking home is much more fun than drunk driving home, and much less dangerous. For instance, if you knock over something driving home, you are screwed; if you knock over something while drunk walking home, everyone cheers.

487. Two men may never, ever meet to eat dinner together any place other than a fast-food restaurant. Find a third, no matter what you have to do . . . or go to a strip club for the buffet.

488. If you take cream and sugar with your coffee, say "cream and sugar." Ordering your coffee "light and sweet" is tantamount to saying "I cried during *Dirty Dancing*."

489. One man may not feed another man any food . . . ever.

490. No man may ever order a sandwich that contains "windswept greens."

491. A man must always average one shower per day. Hence, if a man showers twice two days in a row, he must not shower for the next two days. There is no circumstance grave enough to warrant taking three showers in one day.

492. No man ever complains of being "stressed." Stress is for women.

493. When you're ordering at the drive-thru, if your buddy leans over your lap to order out the window, punch him in the face and then cancel his order.

494. If you have ever read *Men Are from Mars, Women Are from Venus*, then you are from Venus.

495. Unless you are taking pictures of nude models, never own a camera bigger than a Quarter Pounder.

496. Only use an umbrella when absolutely necessary. In fact, using an umbrella at all is really pretty questionable. Whatever you do, if you must use an umbrella, make sure it is black.

497. If you have ever tucked your dick in between your legs and looked in a full-length mirror (a.k.a. the Buffalo Bill), *Never under any circumstances tell anyone.* There is no drug or drink strong enough to excuse that type of behavior.

498. You may never take a bath with bubbles unless there is a chick in it with you. If her boobs are big enough to float on top of the water, then another bath is allowed alone later.

499. Exercising on the elliptical machine is fine, so long as you bring a water bottle to capture the sweat from your dripping vagina.

500. Don't be one of those guys who is overly complimentary of girls with middling attractiveness at best. We all bear the consequences when they strut down the center of the bar with pork-loined shoulders bouncing.

501. At no time can a bobble-head doll occupy your house unless it is of you. If you have your own bobble-head doll then, well, you probably have no need for this damn book, but thanks for the royalties.

502. If a man ever turns to you and says, "Are you sure my shirt isn't going to clash with my shoelaces?" you need to get out of that house in a hurry.

503. Don't ever apologize for sending the air hockey puck soaring off the table in the midst of a highly competitive game, even if it strikes a small child. Reconsider if the small child is Mike Tyson's.

504. Under no circumstances can two men ever ride a motorcycle together.

505. Unless he is either a pimp or dressing up as Abraham Lincoln for Halloween, a man may never wear a stovepipe hat.

506. If one man wears a pink shirt or pink tie, then no other man in his company can also be wearing a pink shirt or a pink tie. If you are not sure whether something is red or pink, this means it is definitely pink.

507. Two men in public may never be consuming either a Popsicle or a banana at the same time.

508. Only wear your old Starter jackets when you are home alone, the heat is broken in your house, and the only blanket you have to cover yourself is the comforter you are knitting.

509. At Christmas, if you see a man wearing a jingle bell on a string around his neck, you are permitted to choke him to within an inch of his life.

510. Even if it seems like a good idea at the time, never push a girl's breasts together to make them look like they are hands clapping.

511. A man signs his name or writes nothing at all; he never uses a closing greeting in an e-mail. In particular, use of the phrases: "I love you," "toodles," and "ta-ta," are all punishable by dick-whipping.

512. Unless he has a starring role in a Hollywood block-buster, a man may never dye his hair a different color.

513. If you dye your hair a different color, next time you are out at the bar, feel free to break a beer bottle on one of your friends' heads. They clearly aren't really your friends if they let you dye your hair.

514. Never put bunny ears behind someone's head in a picture. If a man puts bunny ear's behind your head,

you have legal right to his wife, and his firstborn son may become your serf.

515. Accept that momma jokes officially died as viable burns the moment *White Men Can't Jump* was released. Note: this rule means that despite banging Lindsay Lohan, Wilmer Valderrama is not a man.

516. No matter how much you wonder about how tall you would be in high heels, a man may never try them on.

517. A man may never giggle while running through a sprinkler system.

518. If you have a regular brand of shampoo, and you aren't being paid to endorse the product, give it up and buy what's cheapest.

519. Only one article of alma mater paraphernalia allowed per body simultaneously, unless actually at said alma mater's sporting event, in which case two is a maximum. Body paint counts double.

520. Anyone seen wearing jean shorts, boots, and a wife beater is either coming from or going to jail. Do not harass.

521. Do not cheer loudly at a sports pub if your team is the minority there. This goes triple for European soccer matches. You will most certainly be glassed, stomped, and violently removed from the bar. Once on the street, feel free to taunt if you can still run.

522. Most travel requires only one duffel bag. Fancy suit-cases are not allowed. Folding is not allowed. Throw clothes in duffel bag and go.

523. Never purchase any clothing that is "form-fitting."

524. No man may ever be afraid to ride any roller coaster, even if is called the Guillotine and has a higher ca-sualty rate than the war in Iraq. If you are truly a pansy and must avoid riding a roller coaster, follow this schematic.

    (1) Stand in line until you reach the roller coaster.

    (2) Just before climbing on board, scan the area around the roller coaster for all young children. Inevitably, a kid always chickens out right at the start of the ride. Gallantly offer to stay behind with the child and allow your girlfriend and the saddened par-ent to ride. Wave morosely as the roller coaster leaves you behind. Not only will you avoid mak-ing your pansiness well known, but as a bonus your girlfriend will have rampant and wild sex with you later that night, because you have fooled her into believing that you are a selfless adult with an overflowing fount of maturity. This will be a lie . . . but it will be great sex.

525. The best way to avoid a DUI: If a picture of Jenna Jameson naked can't give you a boner, you are way too drunk to drive home.

526. If you currently have frosted blond tips in your hair, do one of two things:

    (1) Go back to Europe, or
    (2) Wear a burka.

527. The only place someone can walk in with a gun visible and not get mercilessly mowed down is a pawnshop. This speaks volumes about pawnshops. Do not go to pawnshops alone.

528. Never admit that your favorite Smurf was Hefty or that you secretly envied his tattoo.

529. Mesh shorts, not shirts. Pay attention to your vowels. One misplaced vowel can lead to a gym class of sheer terror.

530. If ever caught in a rainstorm, you must walk steadily at the same pace, allowing the rain to soak you. Using a briefcase or newspaper as a substitute umbrella is acceptable. Never run scared through the rain, face winced in fear of the tiny droplets. If you see another man doing this, you should trip him, then repeatedly splash gutter water into his mouth and eyes.

531. A man may not self-assign a nickname; if he does, he shall henceforth be referred to as "Cupcake."

532. Never hook a live baitfish through the bottom.

533. If there is anyone else in the car, then no, you may not sing along. Exception: unless it is the *Dawson's Creek* theme, in which case everyone must sing along.

534. If you're not Latino, it doesn't mean you're not cool, but it does mean you can't drive a purple low rider with flames painted up the sides.

535. If you must get a tattoo, no ink color other than black may be used, unless it is the traditional "mother" tattoo, which is totally tubular.

536. When wearing a polo shirt, if you're thinking about popping up your collar for social use, why not just rip your penis off and stick it to your shoulder instead? This will be less offensive to the general population.

537. Ring pops were awesome. But here's the deal, you can't have a ring pop in public anymore. Having said that, we once heard somewhere or somehow that ring pops come in unmarked boxes if you order them online. So, you know, people might not know if you consumed them in the privacy of your own home while you watch *Teen Wolf*.

538. Doing laundry is sometimes necessary, but is never an excuse to skip a night out at the bar.

539. Even if you have no earthly idea where the softball or baseball is in the air, a man may never cover his own head with the glove and squeal.

540. Should one of your buddies ever utter the phrase, "It's just really tough because I love her so much," while engaged in conversation with you, pretend you didn't hear and change the subject. If he brings it up again, insist on a trip to the strip club.

541. The following exercises are never to be done in public: star jumps and squat thrusts. If you see another man doing these exercises, you have just learned who you should challenge to your next fight.

542. A man never turns down the opportunity to do a keg-stand, funnel a beer, or skinny-dip . . . with women.

543. If your girlfriend has sex with you while wearing a bra, and you aren't a guest star on *Sex and the City*, get a new girlfriend.

544. Unless making a living as a hand or foot model, a man may not receive either a manicure or a pedicure. Incidentally, if you make a living as either a hand or foot model, get a real job.

545. Accept that every time you have cybersex, there are two dicks involved.

546. Don't ridicule the effectiveness of porn spam until you have graduated from college, work in an office, and are tired before Letterman or Leno. Then, you'll see why it is so effective.

547. If you are playing poker with the guys, it is never okay to admit that you don't know how to play a certain type of game. For example, if the dealer says, "We're playing High Chicago, do you know how to play?" never respond with a no. Simply say, "I've only played it a few times, so explain it again." This doesn't admit that you don't know the game yet you can still figure out the rules and prevent yourself from losing more money. Expect your friends to make fun of you, regardless.

548. Repeat after us, a replica of a guillotine is not an appropriate wedding gift.

549. Kicking or punching a dog is never cool. Having said that, if a cat starts annoying you, feel free to grab that thing and punt it across the yard like Reggie Roby. After all, the cat has nine lives and, if he's cool, he's wearing a football helmet.

550. Do not boast to women your proficiency in any of the following:

- Ultimate Frisbee
- Frisbee golf
- Any sport using a Frisbee
- Ping-Pong
- Halo
- Halo 2

551. There's always some guy who wears shorts as soon as it turns forty degrees because, "It's not that cold." Don't be this guy.

552. Puns are, in general, forbidden.

553. If you have seen a male friend within the past week, there is no reason to have a telephone conversation with him, unless the conversation is limited to:

    • How hot a particular female is and strategies on how to bed said female
    • A specific scheme related to making money
    • Making plans for working out/drinking (this conversation should not last longer than forty-five seconds)
    • Arguments about whose cookie-selling Girl Scout would be hotter in five years

554. Don't get a tattoo with a woman's name, because that bitch will cheat on you and you'll have to change that tattoo into a tribal band. And then you'll be a tool.

555. Never wear a leather jacket unless you are willing to deal with the consequences, which include mandatory bar-fights and your friends making *Grease* references.

556. Don't keep a calendar or datebook. Write it on your hand.

557. You may get coffee from Starbucks, but put it in a plain cup and tell people, "I like it stronger than horse piss."

IV.

Sports

My game is like the Pythagorean theorem: it has no answer.
> —Shaquille O'Neal

The day you take complete responsibility for yourself, the day you stop making any excuses, that's the day you start to the top.
> —O.J. Simpson

There are two kinds of Homo sapiens with penises in this world. Those who would wear knee pads and those who would never wear knee pads no matter what. It's important to pick your side. Those who would wear knee pads are all about cushioning the falls of life and making it easier to gently fellate each other on grass lawns as autumn leaves tumble about them. Then there are those men who are willing to be bruised, to suffer the slings and arrows of life and never complain. The latter are men who would never consider wearing knee pads; the former, you need not concern yourself with. The *Man: The Book* Revolution uniforms will not feature knee pads.

Sports for the *Man: The Book* man are like this as well. You're either a sports fan or you're a girl. It's that simple. We're sure there are all sorts of reasons why your philatelic collection or your *Star Trek* conventions make it impossible for you to keep up with sports. They're probably similar to the excuses you make when you hold up your limp penis between your index finger and your thumb and explain why the blood flow to your penis is constrained. Spare us, please. Keep wasting your pathetic seed on pinup photos of Xena Warrior Princess and don't bother us with your petty tripe.

For the rest of us, it's important not to be that guy at sporting events who talks loudly on his cell phone about his job or shakes pom-poms while pretending not to be checking out the ass of every guy who walks by in blue jeans. At the very least, it's important to understand when you can wear an ankle brace and how frequently you should talk trash. Or how you should talk about sports with women or how many beers are too many (wait, we all know this is one of those tricky "Do you still beat your wife questions?" with no right answer).

Basically, we want you to be a sports fan who doesn't make us want to impale you on the nearest flagpole outside the stadium. The kind of guy who doesn't rush home from a game and log onto his mother's computer and head straight to his message board to burnish his keyboard cred. Meanwhile, this guy's mother is banging on the door saying things like, "Milton, your macaroni and cheese is getting cold." We don't want you to be like Milton. We want you to join us in the *Man: The Book* revolution and never even think about wearing a sports jersey anywhere but to or from the stadium. Read on . . . unless your mac and cheese is getting cold, you pussy.

558. A man works out for two reasons:

    (1) To impress women

    (2) To be able to some day end a bar fight by grab-bing a guy and lifting him a foot off the ground by the neck with one hand.

559. When playing mailbox baseball, keep in mind that a swing and a miss can result in your own car getting hit. Make sure the batter has some skill.

560. If your method of swimming may be described as the "doggy paddle," there is no reason for you to ever enter water above your head.

561. In the gym, whenever too many basketballs are stuck in the net, it's a requirement to yell, "Too many balls in the hole!" This, however, is not suitable be-havior to be carried over into the postgame showers.

562. When playing in your company's coed softball league, a man must *always* try to hit the ball over the fence. It doesn't matter if it is an automatic out. Never know-ingly attempt to bunt or just get a base hit—leave that shit to the girls on your team, you little bitch.

563. Once during the football season, a man is allowed a bye-week, where he may choose to not watch any college or NFL games for the whole weekend. Spelling is important: a bi-week, which is when a man chooses to try out sex with another man for seven days, is not the same thing at all.

564. When playing pickup basketball, remember the number two:

- The number of shots you have to hit in a row to be on fire
- The number of screens you are allowed to set per day
- The number of fists upside your head you will receive if you violate the previous rule
- The number of arms raised if any 3-point *game winners* are hit
- The number of stretches you are allowed before starting
- The number of support braces allowed combined with accessories (e.g., wrist/head bands, Iverson sleeves, etc.)
- The number of games won in a row to be "king of the court"

565. This goes without saying: Any trip to the driving range results in a contest. Acceptable contests include:

- Longest drive
- Closest to a predetermined object (flag, tree, staff member, etc.)
- Most drives completed in a certain amount of time (although this one is dumb, since you pay for the golf balls)

566. Always be prepared to pull off *the "Look Away"*: This is to be used when caught staring at a much larger man than yourself bench-pressing weight that you can only dream of.

567. When heading to the driving range, you may bring a maximum of three of your own clubs for use in hitting. (This collection may not include a pitching or sand wedge.) Any more than that, and you are either a tool or a professional golfer. If you see someone at the driving range with his whole golf bag behind him, it is acceptable to challenge this person to a pitching-wedge distance duel. Whoever loses has to give the other his remaining balls (pun intended).

568. If you strike out in a softball game, you buy all drinks for the evening up to $100.

569. When playing intramural basketball, you are hereby entitled to shoot from anywhere at any time, regardless of ability. If an airball ensues, immediately turn to the referee and demand the foul call.

570. Admit that Tecmo Super Bowl was the greatest video game ever created and stop arguing otherwise.

571. If you are not benching in excess of 225 pounds, at no point in time may you grunt in the gym.

572. Unless you are truly unable to afford purchased meat, admit that shooting any animal is really just loud entertainment.

573. Ping-Pong is more than a metaphor for life, it is life itself.

574. It's okay in RBI Baseball or any other baseball video game to insist that no junk pitches are allowed.

575. When playing recreational league softball, being thrown out at first base from the outfield is unacceptable. Scour the rule book. Next at bat, request a motor scooter, claiming a weight handicap. If denied, never pick up a bat until your fat ass can beat out a lob from right field. If this is an impossibility, for every fat ass out, you must homer.

576. Any Madden football game: Fourth quarter. Down by six. Third and twenty. Run the corner route.

577. A man may wear John Stockton shorts for laughs on the basketball court for exactly three minutes fourteen seconds, then he must change.

578. Generally, talent in sports is to be favored; this is not the case, however, with croquet or badminton.

579. It's always funny on a burnout bench press set at the gym, to wait until your buddy is completely burned out and is pinned beneath the bar to exclaim: "Explode!"

580. Trash can Basketball:

     (1) A man must make sure his trash can is at least five feet away from his desk at all times. Placing a trash can underneath or directly beside a desk is unacceptable and cause for ridicule.

     (2) When the trash can is properly located, a man must dispose of all items from his desk, or make a concerted effort to distance himself from the trash can.

(3) If you attempt to throw a piece of garbage into the wastebasket from across the room and miss, you must immediately go pick up the item and walk back to shoot it again from the same location, repeating until successful. Once you sink it, celebrate loudly.

(4) Trick shots are encouraged and awarded extra points.

(5) A bank shot counts as a miss, and a man must retrieve any banked trash from the garbage to reshoot it, no matter what disgusting liquid was in the trash can with it.

581. It is perfectly normal to contemplate killing your best guy friend after he fakes a video game punt and scores. Actually killing him is, surprisingly, only legal in Nova Scotia.

582. When another man's sports team loses, he gets a grace period of exactly five minutes thirty-two seconds before he may be called. If it is your team, turning off your cell phone for one hour per round of playoff loss is acceptable.

583. Know this: if a healthy percentage of your favorite team's players are not sporting playoff beards, chances are they are going down, maybe even literally. To offset this, you must grow a playoff beard or 'stache to try and even the odds. Remember, gotta support the team.

584. If you are not strong enough to get a ball to the backboard from half-court, never step on the basketball court.

585. Unless it's the Super Bowl, if your team wins without scoring a touchdown, then you really shouldn't be bragging. That's like busting a nut while dry-humping. Yeah, it got the job done, but you didn't really score. Just accept the win with a single, slow, self-deprecating nod.

586. Lifting free weights is a must. Only use Nautilus machines when there is a hottie in the vicinity. This will not impress her, but at least you will be closer to her. No grunting is allowed and, when you leave the machine, jack it up by fifteen pounds. Mock the next occupant for lowering the weight.

587. Unless you are an NCAA or professional athlete, you are allowed no more than one story about your athletic accomplishments per night.

588. At any time, you should be able to acquire any sports score within three minutes. For every thirty-second increment over this amount of time, you owe the asker a beer. (Note: This rule only applies for North American sports featuring men. And not bowling. Or the WNBA.)

589. Pussy magic girl shots are not allowed in a respectable game of horse. Pussy magic girl shots are defined in the same way the Supreme Court defines obscenity:

you know it when you see it. For example, all seated shots are by definition pussy magic girl shots.

590. If you can't name the starting quarterback, the running back, and at least two wide receivers of your "favorite" team, then you are a frontrunner. Frontrunners are like giddy schoolgirl freshmen at a varsity football game . . . and just like them, you are wearing panties.

591. Don't wear lifting gloves to the gym unless you would feel comfortable with the result of taking said gloves off and slapping the largest man in the face with them.

592. It is perfectly acceptable to be late to work because you were waiting to see your team's highlights on *SportsCenter*.

593. If you strike out in a Wiffle ball game, you must drop your bat and squarely face the pitcher. He may then choose to peg you with the Wiffle ball if he so desires.

594. When at a sporting event, under no circumstances is it permissible to throw your beer on an opposing player or fan. Soda, tobacco spit, and urine are all perfectly acceptable but, for the love of God, please do not waste any beer.

595. A man may discuss the size or potential size of another man's penis on just one occasion: when Shaquille O'Neal is playing on television.

596. You never *need* to stretch or warm up for any intra-

mural/rec league game you play in. At most you may take a few seconds of quad stretches, a maximum of five warmup shots/throws before you play. Avoid any stretch that requires you to spread your legs wide and place your head in the direct vicinity of your own crotch. A pulled muscle is a small price to pay to keep your masculinity.

597. If you have not won seven Tour de Frances in a row, with cancer, then do not wear multicolored spandex.

598. Never stand and scream for one of those free shirts they throw into the stands during basketball games. It is most likely a shitty shirt and not worth the loss of your dignity. If you are at a game with your buddy and he stands, screams, and jumps up and down like a jackass to catch one, punch him directly in the nuts. Then continuously throw things at him like your nachos, shoes, butcher knife, etc. Whatever it takes to teach him to stop being such a douche around you.

599. If you are working out at the gym and see a hot chick in spandex and a sports bra running on a treadmill, you are required to use the machine directly behind her for as long as it takes for you to be able to successfully select her ass out of a police lineup.

600. Be careful heckling minor-league baseball players, they have very little to lose and have bats in their hands. Heckle major-league baseball players remorselessly.

601. If you claim to have an "inside source" on any sports message board, odds are you either live with your

mother or haven't had sex in over a year. Actually you're probably having sex with your mother.

602. There is no acceptable reason for you to not set your lineup for Fantasy Football. Don't be the asshole who starts Shaun Alexander even though he's been hurt for three weeks. No one likes that guy.

603. A man must be able to hit a golf ball farther than he can throw it. If not, he has to carry someone else's golf bag, as well.

604. If someone from your school is playing on TV, it is completely acceptable to make up a random story about them, so long as it's funny or there was a hot chick involved.

605. A man may not wear wristbands unless he is actually participating in a sport.

606. During football season, there are only three things that a man needs to be doing on Sunday:

(1) Watching football

(2) Watching the score of his fantasy football game

(3) Drinking beer

If you are out shopping on Sunday you better be shopping for either:

(1) A bigger TV to watch football

(2) A faster computer to watch the scores for your fantasy football team

(3) More beer

(4) A new dress and heels, because you aren't a man anymore

607. No matter how great your sports team is, every team has a player who is indefensible when someone makes fun of him. Think Manu Ginobili. Accept this.

608. If you are watching a game in which you played against one of the players in high school, you are allowed one "Story of Glory" about this player per game. Anything more than that, and you sound like a knob and your friends should make fun of you without mercy. There is a reason that tens of thousands of people don't pay to watch you play flag football, assbag.

609. Anytime you see someone wearing a sports jersey and not attending a sporting event, it is always funny to tap your friend and say, "Hey, [*insert player's name on jersey here*]'s at [*insert location*]." For example if you see a guy wearing a Ron Artest jersey at the Subway, you'd say "Hey, Ron Artest's at the Subway." Trust us, this never gets old.

610. Should one of the hot cart girls on a golf course keel over from heatstroke in your presence, the mouth-to-mouth resuscitation may be performed in this order:

(1) The married guy gets first dibs.

(2) The guy with the ugliest girlfriend gets second dibs.

(3) The guy who ordinarily trembles at the thought of speaking to a girl gets third dibs.

(4) At no point is knowledge of CPR to be considered.

611. If one man breaks another man's video game controller, he is obligated to purchase both a new controller and a new game of the owner's choice for the damages inherent in only having one controller.

612. Aside from boxing, any "sport" where the winner is determined by marks from a panel of judges is not a sport. It's a talent show.

613. The only condiment required at a sports party is ketchup. Feel free to loot the house if there is none. If you find yourself angry that there is no gourmet dip, then maybe you should use the semen in the back of your silk boxers. Ass pirate.

614. Someone complaining about the price of beer at a game is like someone complaining about the price of lap dances at a strip club. Just shut the fuck up and enjoy the night.

615. Change your fantasy team name every year that you do not win the championship.

616. If your wife or girlfriend ever says while watching football, "I just don't understand why they don't score more touchdowns," you have two possible responses:

(1) Ignore her, or

(2) Reply, "I just don't understand why we don't have sex more."

617. You may compare white NFL receivers only to Ed McCaffrey or Ricky Proehl. Cross-racial comparisons might upset the space-time continuum and cause cataclysmic destruction.

618. When playing basketball, knee pads are strictly forbidden. If playing with someone wearing knee pads you can never pass them the ball.

619. If you see a professional athlete out at a bar, it is never acceptable to buy him a shot. He makes about seven thousand times more money than you do. Conversely, if you see a professional cheerleader out at a bar, you should spend every last dollar in your bank account, buying her shots.

620. In sports, always pick the guy wearing the jean shorts last.

621. While dribbling in pickup basketball, if you find yourself making the "stop sign" gesture with your off hand to ward off your defender, cease dribbling, hand the defender the ball, and excuse yourself from the game.

622. It is always acceptable when you see two men playing badminton, to laugh, point at them, and exclaim, "Those guys are playing some bad mitten."

623. If it involves ice skates but not pissed off, toothless Canadians with sticks, you sure as shit better not be watching it.

624. Gambling is a sport because it involves blood, sweat, and tears no matter whether you win or lose. Since farting when you have to take a real bad shit is gambling, then shitting is a sport as well. But if your shit involves blood, sweat, and tears, then you really need to get checked out.

625. If someone invites you to a game and then won't drink any beer because it's "not a microbrew" and won't eat a hotdog because he is on a diet, it is okay to ditch him to find another seat. You don't want to have to listen to him talk about his wife's venereal diseases she got screwing another guy during the game, anyway.

626. Unless you are training for the Heavyweight Championship of the World, there is never any reason for you to be jumping rope.

627. You may never call the following fouls/violations in a pickup basketball game: over the back, three seconds, or illegal defense.

628. When golfing, a man gets one floating mulligan. Said floating mulligan may be applied to any stroke on the golf course but may not be used more than once. If the man is wearing one of those golfing caps with a doily on the top, feel free to disregard this rule.

629. We don't care what time of year it is, never wear a Santa hat of your favorite team. Never.

630. Every man should know his forty-time within .1 seconds.

631. Unacceptable topic of conversation during a football game: who Paris Hilton, Pamela Anderson, or Britney Spears is currently dating. Acceptable topic of conversation during a football game: whether you should watch the Paris Hilton, Pamela Anderson, or Britney Spears sex tapes during halftime.

632. If you miss your team's regular season football game, there'd better be a death. If it is a playoff or bowl game, there are no exceptions.

633. Any football explanation beyond, "On offense you try not to be tackled; on defense you try to tackle," is truly wasted on a woman.

634. If you can't tell if a woman is hot or not in her uniform, then it isn't a sport you should be watching. This means the only acceptable sports to watch women play are beach volleyball, tennis, and stripping.

635. Any sport is better when played with beer, but the following sports *must* be played with beer:
    - Badminton
    - Horseshoes
    - Croquet

- Bowling
- Softball

636. If you are playing pickup basketball and wearing an ankle brace, you have to be at least twice as good as the worst player on the court.

637. As of the year 1989, high tens are completely unjustifiable. If someone attempts to give you one, head-butt them directly in the nasal passage.

638. If you wear the jersey of a player who was traded, cut, or left the team via free agency, you deserve all the heckling you get.

639. If you are playing a man in Ping-Pong and he beats you with each hand, you may never again challenge this man to a match.

640. Do not afford intramural basketball referees any respect. They are simply older dorm resident assistants who like whistles.

641. Every time hockey is on television, it is a fair topic to ask why each team doesn't just compete to find the fattest man alive to play goalie.

642. If you need a spot while doing squats, lessen your weight and protect your heterosexuality.

643. No matter how hard you try to finesse-pause it, that DVR strip is always going to partially block the exposed cleavage you're trying to check out during televised sporting events. But just to be sure you should definitely stand directly in front of the television and try to look down behind it.

644. Just remember, there is no conversation worth having at the gym with any man you don't know that takes longer than, "Need a spot?"

645. If a girl will play video games with you while she is naked, you should marry her.

646. Put this one in your back pocket for the next time you hit on NFL cheerleaders: Ninety percent of them are legitimately confused about why their team doesn't have that yellow first-down stripe like everyone else does. Answer this question and you two can play just the tip later that night.

647. A man who is not a referee may not wear a whistle around his neck unless his first name is Sergeant and his last name is Slaughter.

648. Trust us, blow jobs while your favorite team is playing football are about as welcome as eating spicy buffalo wings when you're lost in the Sahara desert. Shit makes no sense.

649. If you are a father, and your eight-year-old son scrapes his knee while playing outside, do not apply a Band-

Aid or any sort of soothing salve. Instead, apply rubbing alcohol and dock a night of television from him for every tear shed. This will make him a very good linebacker.

650. Drawing a charge in pickup basketball is like buying a whore a diamond ring.

651. Any time a sports announcer uses a word you don't recognize (that turns out to be a legitimate word), punch yourself in the balls while wearing three socks. God, why are you so stupid?

652. When playing flag football, accidentally grabbing someone's junk or ass cannot be avoided. Subsequent eye contact can. Nervous laughter and genuine apologies are also plausible responses. But that feeling will still be on your hand, and that's gross.

653. If you throw like a girl, never throw. If you aren't certain whether you throw like a girl and another man has ever laughed when he saw you throwing anything, you should be certain . . . that you throw like a girl.

654. Men who have not commenced skiing before puberty are never required to do anything at a ski lodge but sit in the Jacuzzi and drink beer.

655. Not that we've ever done this . . . but we've heard rolling up socks into a ball, framing your cock and balls, and taking turns throwing the balled-up socks at each other from forty feet away is actually a pretty

good way to build intestinal fortitude. This is called a "cock-duel." First man to tap out buys drinks all night.

656. While we have not tested this at our laboratories, we believe only good things can come from mixing Creatine or other muscle-building supplements into your infant son's baby formula.

657. If the absolute pinnacle of your jump allows you to touch anything less than the rim, there is no point in your jumping in front of other people.

658. Everybody has at least one friend with very questionable hands when it comes to catching. When playing sports, feel free to call this friend "Hands."

659. You are never too old or too tall to engage in a spirited game of six-foot basketball on one of those mini-indoor goals. Swats so violent they break your wife's china are encouraged.

660. Don't be the guy who pretends to like sunflower seeds. Dude, admit that you hate them. Or admit that you secretly crave the luscious scent and taste of sweaty balls.

661. Unless they come with groupies' phone numbers, once you pass the age of eighteen you can't ask another man for his autograph. This is just so demeaning. You might as well hand this man your wife, as well.

662. If you live in the city, freely lie about the distance you can kick a field goal. Even if you've never kicked a football before. Honestly, there aren't that many football fields in cities and it's going to be really hard for somebody to call you on your lie.

663. Within ten minutes of arriving at a sporting event, you must select your first round draft pick in the Cheerleader-I-Would-Bone Draft. Said selection may then be ridiculed or endorsed by your seat companion. This is the case even if you are in the last row of seats in the upper deck and don't have binoculars. Or for that matter, even if you are in the blimp. Beware, Sam Bowie once looked like a solid selection, too.

664. Some men play soccer without shin guards. Do not pick fights with these men. Especially if they are Middle Eastern. Just trust us.

665. Is the guy sitting next to you at a sporting event a complete asshole? Make false friends with him and offer to buy a beer. Then go into the bathroom and fill his cup one-third full of urine. Smile and give it to him when you return.

666. Keep tediously accurate stats when playing any recreational sport. In softball, keep strike-outs-per-inning and slugging percentage. In basketball, keep assist to turnover ratio, blocks per game, and charges taken. Bonus points awarded for procuring an actual card of yourself replete with yearly stats on the back.

667. Whenever girls are playing field hockey, you have to try and look up their skirts. You never know, maybe some girls do play without panties. What do you have to lose?

668. Never go jogging with a woman unless you have already completed eight marathons. Seriously, you have nothing to gain and everything to lose. Most women can run much longer than your fat, lazy ass can.

669. Don't worry, every man has secretly thought the balance beam routine would be much more exciting if there was a large dildo to land on halfway through.

670. But *not* everyone has tried on one of those pink leotards with silver stars on the shoulder and tried to stick his landing in the apartment hallway. You sick fuck.

671. Respect another man's call when he says he's "going dark." This occurs whenever one man says to another, "I'm going dark." It could mean one of two things: either he's recording a sporting event and won't watch it until later and doesn't want you to spoil the outcome, or he's trying to have sex with a black woman. Either is an admirable goal.

672. Even if you work out in the condo pool, never, ever exercise just treading water in the deep end. This looks weird, really weird. You are never having sex with anyone in your complex if you do this.

673. Bring back Smear the Queer at office picnics.

674. Avoid guarding the girl in a basketball game. It's a no-win situation. If you "D" her up, and get in a block or two, you will instantly receive the sarcastic, "Oooooo, you're so good, you blocked a girl" comments from your male friends. On the other hand, if you give up any more than a lucky basket to her, you are forever the guy who got schooled by the girl. Faking an ankle injury is a permissible way to avoid this unenviable position.

675. Anytime you sit where an athletic trainer can hear you and a player is injured, scream, "He needs his groin massaged, get on it! Get on the groin!"

676. If you go bowling and halfway through notice your date isn't wearing any panties, make sure she stands in front of the air vents and gives everyone else a show. Even if she doesn't realize it. Then bang her in the inevitably closed bowling pro shop. Make a joke about your fingers fitting just right in her hole. Afterward, be a nice guy and buy her nachos.

677. Feel free to manage your life as if you are a general manager of an NFL team; this means, with both running backs and women, younger is always better.

678. Occasionally, apropos of nothing, put on a football helmet and spend all day wearing it in your office. When people ask you what you're doing say, "Just wearing a football helmet."

679. Even if someone at the gym is bench-pressing a Miata and you can barely curl a ten-pound barbell, there's never been any weight being benched you weren't confident you could spot.

680. Having sex in the bathroom of a stadium, arena, or gym is pretty impressive. You can feel justified in strutting about for several days. But remember, that's how Magic Johnson got AIDS.

681. If you ever strike out in softball swinging, grate your face against the chain link fence. If you ever strike out looking, an argument with the umpire must ensue. Kick dirt on the plate and tell him to call it both ways.

682. Crowd the plate during rec-league softball games. Dare the pitcher to brush you off the plate menacingly with your bat. When hit, slowly take your base, and stare at any and all opposing players the entire length of the first base line, while repeatedly inquiring if they want some. Taped wrists and unstrapped batting gloves add to the effect.

683. Admit it to us, we won't judge you, you owned that CD *Jock Jams*, didn't you? What, you didn't? Really? Yeah, neither did we.

684. Men who are not die-hard fans of one NFL team should be looked upon with suspicion and scorn.

685. Knowing is half the battle. So, for the record, it's *not* cool to ask an NFL quarterback if you can tickle his

balls next time you're dp'ing some random chick together.

686. Everybody played G.I. Joe football with the little paper football clutched in the Joes' players hands. Not everyone still plays. Stop now.

687. Arena football cheerleaders are the porn stars of the professional cheerleading universe. They'll do it dirty, they'll do it raw, and they'll do it on tape. Trust us, they have no shame. So go ahead and sing along to the "Hey" song while slapping your dick on their forehead.

688. The "illegal touching" penalty and "tight end" jokes can only be used once per party. The second person to use them has to take a Copenhagen fine-cut dip for at least the duration of the drink of the slowest drinker. (Note: If the slowest drinker is slower than seventeen minutes, then he must trade his drink for the dip.)

689. During a basketball game, yell, "Shuttlecock!!!" before any and all shots your man takes. This will definitely put his shot off, and most likely draw his ire. If anyone on the court knows what one is, sub them immediately. You *can* know too much.

690. Unless you've been paid millions of dollars to star in a romantic comedy or have children, there's no reason you should ever be on a playground swing set.

691. "Hey, nice pole!" "Wow, that's a great rod!" . . . unfortunately, there is just no appropriate way to compliment another man on his fishing gear.

692. Pulled-pork nachos are the manliest possible food at a sporting event. This means, no matter where you are or what the menu is, demand that you be served pulled-pork nachos when you reach the front of the refreshment line.

693. The day your favorite player can be a kicker is the day when he can consistently make field goals off the uprights, because that shit is cool. And if you haven't ever lost a game off a banked field goal off the uprights in Tecmo Super Bowl, then put down this book and leave the store. Now.

694. If you throw any type of ball and it hits another man in the face in the midst of a game, never apologize. Men were made to catch balls. Of course, juggling balls at any time is strictly forbidden.

695. Men leave their seats to purchase overpriced hotdogs during halftime of college football games. Women stay to watch the marching bands. Keep this in mind next time you're humming along to Hail to the Victor in your new frilly lace panties.

696. If you have courtside seats to a basketball game, it is mandatory that you heckle the opposing team's best player without mercy. However, don't be sur-

prised if this player beats you soundly at some point during the game, as he can most definitely hear your verbal jabs. If he assaults you, foresake all defense and adopt the fetal position. Later, claim you were defending an unseen infant from the player's unprovoked wrath. This will make a good story to tell at the next card game with the fellas.

697. Breaking up a fight between two naked men in a locker room or prison shower is completely off limits. Let those two naked gladiators have at it. This will prevent you from any accidental contact with unclothed male genitalia.

698. It is a must to spend more money on beer than the actual cost of your ticket. If the beer is free at the game, then you must sneak in.

699. The number of seat cushions on a couch is the maximum number of people allowed to sit on it while watching a game. If there is a loveseat, leave that fucker empty. Sit on a folding chair or floor if need be, but no crowding is allowed. Any violation draws a "too many men on the field" penalty, and the offending party must stand or be the beer bitch for the remainder of the period in progress or at the discretion of the host.

700. Talking "trash," "smack," or "shit" while engaging in a sport is a trustworthy sign of healthy levels of testosterone. If you have not reached the level of a "fake

fight" during a basketball game within the last year, start one in your next game (A "fake fight" is one where you bump chests and just stare at each other for a few seconds with no intention of fighting or, if separated by at least two players on your team, you spread your arms with the "I'm right here if you want me" expression, again, with no intention of fighting). Sometimes, just for the hell of it, elbow the fat guy in the gut while posting him up.

701. There is no reason to stare intently at the huddle, unless you like ogling at men in white, sweaty, spandex pants. Paying attention to substitution patterns? Please, you need to substitute your gaping vagina for a dick and balls.

702. Unless playing for money, do not kick field goals in video game football. Any win in which the victor kicked a field goal may be deemed illegitimate.

703. Every time a sideline reporter comes on television, take a shot. Every time she is below a 7 on the hotness scale, take another. This is the only way to make sideline reporters relevant. Women on the sidelines should be called "cheerleaders" and, like children in the nineteenth century, be seen and not heard.

704. Special teams players are like the bouncers of the NFL: they are huge, crazy, will do anything for a job, and feel no pain. Do not ever provoke them, they will eagerly disembowel you right there in the stadium.

705. In paper football, the edge of the table means the edge of the table. If you wanted to make it easy to score touchdowns, you could have played video games.

706. One of your lifelong dreams should be to ride in the Goodyear blimp over a game. If not, your goals are way, way, way too low.

707. Winning a game in a particular sport and winning a video game version of the same sport are on an equal level, and both allow for the same amount of taunting.

708. There is no liquid, absolutely none, that should be consumed at a sports party, other than beer or liquor.

709. If, during an argument in the game, a friend uses the phrase, "If I was a betting man . . ." then he is not a bettor, which makes him not a man.

710. If you ever break your arm while arm-wrestling, don't admit it. Just pretend the cracking noise was a fart and go cry in the men's room.

711. Anytime you explain to a woman the parameters of your sports bet and the reason you are destined to win, you will inevitably lose that bet. Worse, your wife will propound some illogical theory that ends up coming true. This is why you never tell your wives what you are betting on or how much you are betting.

712. It is completely acceptable to be severely disappointed if you discover your team's cheerleaders wear pantyhose during a televised game. This, however, is not just cause for taking down the team cheering calendar, which you masturbate to during "Period Week."

713. Do not boo your team unless you are actually at the game. When you do it at home, this makes you look like a whiny little bitch.

714. You may only watch an instant replay of a disputed call three times. Anything after that, then you are just watching sweaty dudes flex and bounce in slow motion. The beach celebration in *Rocky 3* should have taught you a lesson: slow motion has its perils.

715. They sell beer at baseball games for a reason: to encourage drunk heckling from 450 yards away. The farther you are from the field, the more violent and graphic your taunts should be.

716. You should always feel fairly confident that you can whip a punter or kicker's ass in a bar fight.

717. If any professional athlete sits out a playoff game with an injury, no matter what the injury, you would have played. This remains true even if you have skipped an intramural game because of a stubbed toe.

718. At a sporting event, if you have ever heard another heckler use the phrase before, please spare us all and shut up.

719. Halftime is a great opportunity to try out the first three positions of your newest porn acquisition. Feel free to incorporate sports terminology as necessary. Of course, this assumes you have a willing female with you. More likely, you don't. So, just go ahead and sit on your hand until it gets numb and play "The Stranger" again.

720. Your favorite player cannot have two first names or have a girl's name, or have served time in prison and had stitches to repair his torn asshole.

721. If anybody on your favorite team is seen "dropping salt" (a.k.a. crying), by association, *you* were seen crying. As a penalty, you must drink a beer for the number of seconds equal to the jersey number of your crying team member.

722. At no point can you legitimately *believe* any professional boxer truly sucks at fighting. This is because he would knock your chin through the back of your skull in four seconds, no matter how effeminate he looks in the ring.

723. No man may raise his arms in the air after a made three-point basket in pickup basketball. (Since two of our authors played D-1 basketball for Colorado we have split opinions on this. Surprise, surprise the white guy, JT, is for it.)

724. If your heckling doesn't contain either profanity or foul language, it is merely a verbal jab. Verbal jabs are gay.

725. If your buddy insists he can bench-press any weight and upon your spot said buddy immediately pins himself with said weight, you may spend thirty seconds mocking his weakness before you have to assist him.

726. If you've ever wondered, yes, it is worth tearing your rotator cuff to win a fast-pitch contest at radar measuring games. If you throw slower than sixty miles per hour, feel free to impugn the quality of the radar gun.

727. No man may ever go bowling with the guardrails up.

V.

~~Potpourri~~ AssortMANT

LEBOWSKI: What makes a man? Is it being prepared to do the right thing, whatever the cost? Isn't that what makes a man?
THE DUDE: Sure, that and a pair of testicles.
—The Big Lebowski

You just wait. I'm going to be the biggest Chinese star in the world.
—Bruce Lee

Upon these pages we have done our best to make you a better man. These rules of *Man: The Book* represent the best advice we could bring together for men of all races, creeds, religions, and even Asian people. Trust us, these rules work. Now we have come to that great collection of rules that do not pertain to any particular subset of male interest (sports, bars, women, or manicants). At this point you may feel tired, out of breath, or want to rest your head upon the fertile bosom of the woman sitting next to you on the airplane. Buck up, breathe deeply, and, by all means, dive between those twin pillars of titstasy. When you are back, having been slapped, arrested, or gained a story that will make you the envy of every man on Earth, we implore you to please finish the book. There is still much to be gained; you are not quite ready to be off entirely on your own. Undoubtedly, you may feel an upsurge in confidence, be bedding women by the bushel, and occasionally even be tempted to go back to your favorite pastime of wearing lacy women's panties. We beg you, please complete your *Man: The Book* training.

Remember when Luke fought Vader before he was a Jedi and lost his hand? Right now, you know just enough to be dangerous for yourself. Imagine if you lost your own right hand: how much would this kill your game? Put another way, how many dudes with one hand are with hot chicks? Exactly. So read on, there isn't much remaining now. We promise you that you are close to being a full-fledged *Man: The Book* soldier. Already we can almost see you from the corner of the bar where we are drinking whiskey straight from the bottle with a hot bartender who has just decided that she doesn't like serving us wearing a shirt or bra. We see you, flickering in the distance past the losers with upraised pink drinks and popped collars and wristbands of many colors. We see you but the fat girls are obscuring you now. You're fading. Keep marching, the revolution needs you. Don't fail us now. Onward, men, we must take that bunker.

728. If at any point a porno movie you are watching features two naked men and no naked women, you may watch the movie for thirty seconds before having to admit that your porno selection was horribly flawed.

729. Occasionally it's fun to drive through a rich neighborhood in the middle of the day and scream, "Oh my god, it's the INS!" as loud as you can. Then park and watch the resulting bedlam as nannies, yardmen, and assorted other illegals storm down the streets.

730. Always travel with an ax in your car. Don't ask why, just trust us.

731. Just because you are dressed up as a Civil War–era Confederate soldier, that does not mean you can have sex with any female slave reenactor you so choose. Incidentally, isn't choosing to be a slave reenactor the most ridiculous thing on earth?

732. If your lampshade matches your bed cover and you purchased both, there is a 100 percent chance you don't change the channel when Justin Timberlake comes on.

733. It's not drunk driving if you are on your way to Krystal.

734. If you can lasso anything, you are awesome. Sit on the front porch of your house and attempt to catch fat chicks.

735. If, at any moment, another man catches you watching an animated Disney movie by yourself, he is allowed to exaggerate this fact and claim that you beat off to Ariel from *The Little Mermaid*. In fact, this is probably not even an exaggeration.

736. Ru-486 is so overrated. Conversely, a quick karate chop to the gut is so underrated.

737. If you ever find an unclaimed digital camera, do not return it until you have cycled through every photograph in search of amateur porn. Trust us, it's worth checking.

738. It sucks to be the oldest dude at spring break. But it sucks even more to be the youngest dude at the office.

739. Grad school is like college—except you've graduated. Basically, go to grad school.

740. If you see your five-year-old nephew's hamster and the first thing you think to talk about is the one that supposedly got stuck up Richard Gere's ass, by all means, share the story.

741. No matter how it actually happened, if you lose a finger, toe, arm or leg, blame an alligator. Trust us, even though we don't know anyone this has legitimately happened to, this seems like it will get you more pussy than you can possibly imagine.

742. Upon seeing shit stains in the basin, you have three attempts to power-blast it off while drunkenly pee-ing. After that, you gotta clean it, that's just nasty.

743. Contrary to popular belief, shitting in the potpourri basket will *not* cover up the smell.

744. A man knows Upper Deck is not always a baseball card, and a pearl necklace is not always jewelry.

745. It's only an urban legend that there is dye in the pool that turns red if you piss in it. That was your gon-orrhea. Go get tested, Mr. Sick Dick.

746. Jacking off to hundreds of twelve-second porn clips in a row isn't stupid, because it's free. Plus it builds up your Masturbatory Forty-time for when you only have three minutes until the stewardess gets to your row and serves the meal.

747. Rubbing one out in the friendly skies does not qualify you for the Mile-High Club . . . unless you were in first class.

748. If your son tells you he is gay, lovingly pull him aside and tell him it's okay, as long as he brings over scant-ily clad cheerleaders for slumber parties, where every-one else will dance to Madonna songs without wearing bras.

749. As long as it's not all in pennies or Susie B.'s you can pay for anything in as much change as you want.

750. The ability to quickly scale a chain-link fence like a cop chasing a crackhead is part of the litmus test for manliness. Anyone who has to straddle it like Annie Oakley riding sidesaddle on a pony to get over is immediately deemed a bitch with no balls.

751. When checking out in a grocery line, always put the bananas between two ball-shaped items on the belt to form a rudimentary dick. This is always hilarious and you can never get in trouble for it, unless you actually put your dick and balls on the belt, in which case you are a God.

752. You know you enjoy watching animals have sex, and are secretly jealous they are getting more than you.

753. Taking pictures of your sleeping baby nieces and nephews surrounded by drug, alcohol, and sex paraphernalia is a must. It will teach them a lesson: Never pass out around fucked-up people. After all, this could one day save their life.

754. You officially "can't fight" after getting your ass kicked twice in a four-month period. Or after a string of three losses in a row. This is why you only prey on the weak and fratty. To end the slump, wait until the Dalai Lama visits your town and deck that bastard. Losing streak: over.

755. Unless you are Native American, get that dumb fucking dream catcher off your wall. Girls don't like seeing weird shit like that when they are about to get

naked, which probably explains your case of desert-dick.

756. Hungry, horny, and angry. These are the only feelings men should have. On rare occasions, happiness is found, but only when all three are involved.

757. Watching the disgusting porn someone at work e-mailed to you, with naked girls farting on other girls' faces over and over and over again, is not something you should be ashamed of . . . masturbating to it later that night however in super-slow-motion is something that should be kept to yourself.

758. If it doesn't smell too bad and doesn't have any no-ticeable beer or puke stains on it, then yes, you can wear the shirt you passed out in to work the next day.

759. It's never too early for a father to teach his son about sex. So as soon as your boy can talk, make certain he knows how to say, and appropriately use, the phrases "doggy-style," "donkey punch," and "popping her cherry."

760. No matter what you say publicly, when your dog at-tacks the neighbors or one of their pets, you secretly couldn't be prouder of him.

761. You don't like musicals; there isn't even a basis for an argument otherwise. Make sure to remind your girl of this several times, the next time she makes

you sit through the movie *Chicago*. This should make her feel guilty enough to try something kinky during sex that night. If not, make her sit through the viewing of your newest *Shane's World* porno with you the next night.

762. Being a degenerate gambler is only a problem if you run out of disposable body parts.

763. If, while on the subway, your hand happens to brush against the nice ass of the woman in front of you, follow the "tree falling in the forest" rule: if no one saw you do it, it didn't happen.

764. Music Rules:

(1) Owning or playing CDs by the following artists is permissible only for the purpose of seducing women:
- Tori Amos
- Sarah McLachlan
- Any former *American Idol* contestant

(2) Under no circumstances should the following artists be owned, listened to, or tolerated:
- Kenny G
- Michael Bolton
- John Tesh
- David Hasselhoff
- Ani DiFranco

(3) If a woman makes you listen to Ani DiFranco, your relationship is submitted to a jury of your guy friends, who may decide you are no longer allowed to see this woman.

765. A man may own at most one album by one of the following artists, which he must listen to sarcastically and engage all males present in rapt conversation about how bad it is (as he sings along at the top of his lungs):

- Journey
- Bon Jovi
- Boston
- Poison

766. You must watch all three *Rambo* movies, and all six *Rocky* movies (yes even the fifth). You must never watch *Judge Dredd*, *Cliffhanger*, or *Throw Momma from the Train*. *Tango and Cash* is the only non-Mongoloidish Stallone movie allowed.

767. A man is well aware that if Brandy and Sam Cassell ever had a child, the offspring would truly have eyes in the back of its head.

768. You must own at least three, but preferably all, of the following movies, as they form the canon of man (*not* to be called the Manon, asshole).

- *The Godfather* I, II
- *The Big Lebowski*

- *Scarface*
- *Fight Club*
- *Die Hard* 1-4
- *Every Dirty Harry movie*

769. If your shoe size is equal to or greater than your ACT score and you are not a professional athlete or a rapper, you better be damn good looking.

770. Naming your dog after alcohol, an NBA, NHL, or NFL bad-ass, or a swear word is irrevocably cool. Conversely, if you have a dog that can't whip a cat's ass or kill anything, then give Muffy back to your grandma and find a real pet.

771. If you have a hair-straightener in your bathroom, it had better be for making miniature grilled cheese sandwiches while shitting, showering, or shaving.

772. At some point in your life, you should travel to a mountain region and sprint to the highest mountain peak. Once you've reached the top, hold your hands in the air and scream at the top of your lungs, "DRAGO!!! DRAGOOO!!!!"

773. There is always enough time to hit the snooze button one more time.

774. At some point in your life, you should enter at least one eating contest, arm-wrestling competition, or join a skeet-shooting club.

775. At all times, a man acknowledges that Colin Farrell is having more sex than him.

776. If someone tells a fart joke or story in your presence, fake laugh as hard as you can, then tell the exact same joke or story, replacing the word *fart* with *sneeze*. Then laugh just as hard until the person who told the fart joke leaves.

777. If another man has his eyebrow pierced, feel free to rip it out and slap him with an open-handed palm.

778. Watching porn with other men is only permitted if you are all clothed.

779. All showers must comply with the "two-bottle rule," if a man is not sharing the shower with a female companion. To meet the limits of this rule, remove all bottles not labeled shampoo or that make use of the words *exfoliate* or *soft*.

780. If you have known your male friend for more than two months, and if his car is older than one year, you may openly pick your nose as a passenger, and sprinkle it on the floor.

781. Every man should attend the following sporting events in his life: professional wrestling match, heavyweight championship fight, Super Bowl, Tijuana donkey show, cock fight, Amsterdam's red-light district.

782. If you see someone walking with a bowl cut, a rat tail, a box, or any design shaved in their hair, they are lost and are undoubtedly looking for Jimmy Walker or Joe Dirt. Give them directions. A fight will likely ensue; odds are, they have a butterfly knife or a switchblade. Run.

783. Aim is less important than distance. This applies to most things, but especially to urinals.

784. At least three answers to questions about your life should begin, "Just for the hell of it . . ."

785. All men have a duty to go camping. When camping, the following are expressly forbidden:

   • Mattress pads
   • Pillows
   • Soap
   • Silverware

   A camping man sleeps on the hard ground with a balled-up pile of clothes under his head, and always has filthy hands, which he eats with.

786. Taboo conversation starters while camping:

   • "In Boy Scouts, we used to . . ."
   • "So, is that a tattoo or a birthmark?"
   • "I'm cold—do you think we would be warmer if . . . ?"

787. Help, like emotion, is an option, not a requirement.

788. Travel to Las Vegas (a man's mecca) at least once yearly. However never even think of going to Mecca. Tits? Negligible.

789. Anytime you see/hear a loud motorcycle (a.k.a. hog or chopper), you must look in the direction of it and nod your head approvingly. Crotch rockets are excluded.

790. Try and get a sexual innuendo out of as many sentences as you can. Snicker but don't giggle.

791. Boxer briefs are essentially the male Wonderbra. Ergo, you can only wear these if the woman you are dating is attempting to confuse you about the size of her chest. Which means you can always wear them.

792. When you hear the word *favor*, run, fake a seizure, or hang up.

793. Modified 5-Second Rules for different food items:
    • Potato chip/pretzel: 25 seconds
    • Piece of dry gum: 10 seconds
    • Piece of chewed gum: 2 seconds
    • Buffalo wing: 10 seconds
    • The last buffalo wing: 20 minutes

794. If you're tired at work because you stayed up all night

drinking and/or having sex, inform all of your male co-workers that this is the case and they must cover for you. If you're tired because you were out at the late show of a Meg Ryan movie (not the one where she gets naked, of course), keep it to yourself.

795. Never be bashful when you have to take a dump. Simply announce it to the room, stick the newspaper under your arm, and leave.

796. Always have reading material readily available in all bathrooms at your home. If you visit a buddy and he has nothing to keep you occupied while doing your business, feel free to deposit your fecal matter in the tank of the toilet (also known as "upper decking").

797. A man readily acknowledges that Princess Leia sitting on Jabba's lap was the greatest moment of his preadolescent life.

798. *Slip-and-slides* are a good idea everywhere. Unless they're all male, then you are fulfilling every gay man's fantasy.

799. It is always okay to shamelessly use a friend or family member's puppy or toddler to try to pick up women.

800. If a man has an Italian name, and a New York or New Jersey accent, he should be treated as a member of the Mafia until it can be proven otherwise.

801. A simple high-five can only be utilized on the following occasions:

- During a highly attended sporting event in which you are an actual participant
- During a highly attended sporting event in which you are an incredibly drunk observer and your favorite team just hit a homerun/hit a three-pointer/scored a touchdown to win the game
- While you and a buddy are having rampant, debaucherous sex with Salma Hayek and Jessica Alba at the same time.

802. Remember, no matter what, at work the TPS reports come first.

803. Crapping in the office is a must, at least once a day. Coordinate your session to immediately follow the cleaning crew, so that your experience is a pleasant one. Do not float from stall to stall; rather, once you have found a suitable throne, return to it daily. Whilst seated, do not spend your time idly: Print out your favorite sports column and read it. Play Tetris on your cell phone. Reorganize your wallet.

804. When your boxer briefs become just "boxers," you have an eating disorder.

805. If the only track marks you see are in your briefs, believe it or not, you are actually not doing that bad. This is your best-case scenario when it comes to those two words. Celebrate.

806. "If you don't stand for something, you'll fall for any-
     thing." This is a bullshit platitude. If you aren't stand-
     ing, then you can't fall.

807. You should have a poster of Bruce Lee, *Goodfellas*,
     John Belushi (*not* Jim Belushi) or your favorite foot-
     ball team hanging at some location in your house,
     regardless of your spousal situation.

808. If you know the meaning and relevance of the term
     horticulture, take your balls back from your wife and
     spend at least seventy-two hours away from her, pre-
     ferably in a biker bar of ill repute.

809. Muslim friends are awesome. Make sure you never
     miss an opportunity to tell your buddy, "Muslims are
     the bomb, man."

810. If you have a gay friend, there is nothing wrong with
     having him drop hints to a woman that a completely
     straight man who is vying for her affections is actu-
     ally gay.

811. Don't be afraid to admit that watching pornography
     is better than sex with many ugly women.

812. If you are aware a friend of yours only has one tes-
     ticle, you are entitled to make a single one-testicle
     joke per day.

813. There is nothing funnier than an f-bomb properly placed when telling a story.

814. When driving in rain/snow conditions, if you see pedestrians standing on the sidewalk (regardless of sex or age), it is mandatory to splash any and all of them thoroughly while roaring with laughter, your middle finger extended out the window (also known as the "Streetside Tsunami").

815. When you show any picture of your wife, she must be in a semicompromising position.

816. The speed limit should be broken on all roads at all times. A limited exception exists for ninety-seven-year-old men braking for a group of orphaned baby ducks.

817. If you see a guy with a girl who is inappropriately hot for him, you are permitted to approach him and say, "Nice hottie—are you rich or is she a prostitute?"

818. If you see a car doing a bad parallel-parking job, you must comment audibly, "It's probably a woman."

819. When stuck in a natural disaster with a girl, claim you don't want to die a virgin. If she says yes, she is stupid. If she declines and you survive, tell all your friends she is a bull dyke, but you almost converted her.

820. Paying for a box of condoms, a pack of football cards, a tank of gas, or a porno magazine is not required anytime you can take them without getting caught.

821. There is no place you would rather be right now than a wet T-shirt contest at a high school cheerleading party.

822. Having at least six names for each sexual organ is a must. For any empty spaces, fill in with slang for body excrement. Our favorite for breasts: "chest fruits" . . . classy.

823. If you don't have an "outy," once a year, take some time out to clean your belly button. There's crap in there.

824. Be careful when lighting your own farts: dangerous burning can result.

825. Cock-blocking is only allowed when sisters are involved.

826. If you play poker and wear sunglasses, you'd better not get eliminated from the game in ten minutes. Sure, nobody read your eyes, but everyone can clearly see that you are a tool.

827. The only gratuitous nude scene any man may admit to ever having seen was Kevin Bacon in the shower during *Wild Things*.

828. If you nick yourself while shaving your pubic hair, claim that several girls fought over the right to blow you and this caused your resulting injury. Then cry quietly in the corner.

829. Having hemorrhoids is perfectly normal and doesn't mean that no girl will ever sleep with you again. Wait, yes it does. Dude, you have bloody blisters in your anus; we don't even want you to buy this book.

830. In a group of men helping someone move, the first one to want to rest is immediately ridiculed and forced to continue working while everyone else takes a break.

831. You are only allowed to attend one function per year at which you must dress in a costume. An exemption for a second costume-required function is allowed if it involves a sorority and your date dresses sluttily. Of course, if it is a Halloween party and your date isn't dressing sluttily, you need a new date.

832. Puking under any circumstance is hilarious, and should be appreciated by all with hefty laughter. Unless it is your girlfriend puking at 6:00 A.M. every day; then you are the only one not laughing.

833. Don't be afraid to scratch your crotch in any social situation short of a funeral.

834. If your friend metaphorically has no testicles, feel free to make fun of him endlessly. If he truly has no testicles, try to limit your use of the word *ball* or any other synonym in normal conversation.

835. A man may not intentionally wound, maim, or make fun of a manatee.

836. If you forget the rules of *Man: The Book,* ask your-self this, WWMFD: What would Morgan Freeman do?

837. When visiting a Civil War battlefield, a man must always be photographed standing alongside a cannon.

838. If a male debate cannot be decided by the result of rock, paper, scissors, it is not worth being decided at all.

839. At least 85 percent of your T-shirts should have been free via stealing, borrowing, or begging.

840. "One man's trash is another man's treasure." This is true for everything except women. Think about it.

841. Whenever a group of at least two men are donating blood at the same time, you must make it a competition to see who fills up his bag first.

842. If you've never hired a stripper and watched a drunk buddy fuck one with a dildo mask on his forehead, then you haven't really lived at all. Drop this book and make it happen.

843. When purchasing porn at an airport, it's perfectly normal to pretend to be interested in whatever magazines are closest to the porn. No one wants to be the guy standing in a crowded line to buy *Cum-dumpsters*. Wait until the crowd dissipates and then pounce.

844. It's okay, every time we see a used condom outside a college dorm, we wonder how hot the girl who got screwed was, too.

845. On demand, any man must be able to name five Internet sites that supply free porn. Also, do yourself a favor and subscribe to www.redclouds.com. Trust us, pretty soon you'll feel like redclouds is paying you to masturbate.

846. If you can name two people on *The View*, turn in your balls now. If you have never heard of *The View*, you can have ours.

847. If you ever owned a Tevin Campbell CD, you are allowed to lie about it.

848. [Gross weight of all shoes owned] < [Gross weight of porn collection]*

849. When your car needs to be repaired, you must pretend to know what the mechanic is talking about. It is also a good idea to attempt to give the impression that you would have been able to fix the problem yourself, with the right tools. Appropriate lines to be inserted include:
    - "I tried that myself, but I just don't have enough space in my garage so that's why I had to have you do it."
    - "I fixed that on my Ford F-250 once, I just didn't know how to do it on this little car."

*Add a quarter pound for each gigabyte of computer-based porn.

- "A thousand dollars? I could get the part for a hundred!" [Note: This is usually true.]
- "I tried to fix it but my giant penis and wallet got in the way."

850. If you accidentally hit another man hard enough to make him bleed/bruise/break a bone, a simple nod is an acceptable apology. If you accidentally brush another man's hand, knee, or thigh, a formal written apology, profuse verbal contrition, and a round of beers are required.

851. *The Johnny Cash/Shel Silverstein rule*: If you are a man with a name that is easily mocked (e.g., Sue), you must work out twice as hard as people with normal names, starting at age ten.

852. If a buddy calls you while you're being fellated, you must answer the phone, talk normally, and later tell the calling party about it (as soon as possible, preferably as soon as she leaves to go clean up).

853. Every man should own an outdoor grill and use it at least twice per week. In the case of a weeklong blizzard it is acceptable to use only once per week.

854. If a man asks you what you think of his duvet cover, the only acceptable response is a punch to the face.

855. Unless at a crowded movie theater or sports stadium, you may not choose a urinal directly next to one that is in use. Always skip a space.

856. Do not send your buddy an e-mail forward unless he could get fired for opening it at work.

857. If your buddy sends you an e-mail forward that gets you fired, you have no one to blame but yourself for opening it.

858. A man may only wear turtlenecks if his neck has a huge goiter or he doesn't want his girlfriend to know about the hickey he received from someone else.

859. The wearing of wife-beaters is recommended because a man never knows when his building may be hijacked and his shirt torn off in a deadly struggle with terrorists.

860. Even if you don't know how to use one, all men should claim to be familiar with an ax and a bulldozer.

861. Unless you are a pro athlete, scion of European royalty, or Internet multimillionaire, a stripper on the stage gets no more than one dollar at a time.

862. If making fun of your buddy for being a pussy gets tiresome, feel free to stop . . . and call him a vagina.

863. A man's schedule is rarely predetermined, but instead largely based on necessity. Examples:

   • The only food in my fridge is a slice of cheese and some salsa. Today I go to the grocery store.

- There is a toothpaste stain on my only pair of work pants. Today I go buy some more work pants.
- I have run out of plastic forks. Today I do dishes.
- I broke up with my girlfriend. Today I buy more porn.

864. It is entirely acceptable to purchase gifts the day of the significant event. Cards should be prewritten by Hallmark and need only be signed. Provide a salutation such as "Yours" or "Love" if you are feeling creative.

865. When fixing a hem, remember to make sure the bobbin and the sewing needle have the same color thread—you don't want to have to go back and rip out a seam!

866. If you laugh at a story that is not remotely funny, you have freed the unfunny story teller from mockery and all ridicule is transferred to you.

867. Shower masturbation is permitted, nay, recommended. Please shoot for the drain.

868. If you and your buddies go out and are both wearing the same shirt or hat, the wussier of the two automatically loses the right to wear the matching clothes. If no wuss can be determined, then you will probably get your ass kicked no matter what you are wearing.

869. Because the seven does not look like any other number, do not sully its midsection with a horizontal line. Women can see through shit like that.

870. Midgets are funny and should be treated as such. If possible, befriend a midget and go out dressed in the same clothes, telling every woman you meet that you are twins.

871. If you are forced to attend a movie by yourself, arrive just as the lights go out and sit nowhere near children. Keep your hands well above groin level if it contains nudity.

872. The only time you should stop a friend from fighting is when you realize his opponent has the ability to beat both of you like a trailer park housewife. At this point, hold your friend back and repeat the phrase, "Kicking his ass isn't worth going to jail."

873. If a buddy has accidentally killed a hooker in a foreign country, you must assist him in finding an adequate way to dispose of the body.

874. Not having openly peed in a public place, in blatant and purposeful disregard of the law, is the equivalent of not having reached puberty.

875. If you ever have the opportunity to buy an original General Lee, do not think twice. Mortgage everything you own, if necessary. If you own nothing, steal it.

876. Possessing sensitivity and strictly adhering to the code of *Man: The Book* are not mutually exclusive. For example, consistently feed your pet . . . assuming it's not a cat.

877. If your shoelaces are not white and match any article of clothing you are wearing, do not go out in public. If your shoelaces match your wristbands, do not travel below the Mason-Dixon line.

878. Don't worry, everybody wanted to be Michael Knight.

879. Learn to fully understand and adequately utilize the word *loophole*.

880. Fifty percent of all television channels must be dedicated to sports or porn. Learn to watch no less than eight different shows at once, thus driving your wife or girlfriend insane.

881. If you spill something on a piece of clothing and the stain cannot be removed with some soapy water and a bit of elbow grease, throw it away and buy a new one.

882. A man is always ready to catch an object that is thrown at him. It is perfectly acceptable to toss a breakable object in the general direction of another man, and if it falls and breaks, you may freely blame him and assess him the cost of the damage.

883. If you ever find yourself in a room surrounded by Ninja assassins hell bent on taking your life, remember that Ninjas will only attack one at a time, so plan your counterattack appropriately.

884. If you happen to be walking along the street and come across a $20 bill, the only feasible way to spend this rare gift is on a case of beer and a discreetly rented girl-on-girl porno.

885. Behind every man in prison, there is a much bigger man.

886. Always have the ability to access a free, quality Internet porn site in under one minute.

887. After every binge week, month, or year, a man must take an SOS, otherwise known as a Shower of Solitude, where he thinks of all the bad shit he's done, possible STDs contracted, money blown, and lives wrecked, and pray for forgiveness until the water runs cold (no masturbating allowed, this is serious). This will accomplish two things:

    (1) An SOS confessional is the man equivalent of going to church, and

    (2) You will have showered at least once that week, month, or year.

888. If you see a man with a tattoo on his face or head, turn

and walk away. Oddly enough, he probably doesn't want you staring at it and you definitely can't kick his ass. Nothing can hurt that man.

889. On road trips, men may only call bed partners of other men for the following reasons:

- Someone snores horribly.
- Someone is hugely fat and is known to take up the entire bed.
- Someone is a known cuddler.

890. The next time you get fitted for a suit, wear a cup. This protects your good ol' boys from any accidental brush-bys. If the guy asks you if you are wearing one say, "It's none of your business . . . but my balls are actually made of steel."

891. If you have an Asian friend, it is always funny to occasionally call him "Short-round."

892. Just because Stone Cold Steve Austin can pull off shotgunning a beer and crashing the can into his forehead does not mean your friend from the accounting department can.

893. If you have no idea what the product does, or how to use it, this makes it the perfect wedding gift for a woman. The bride will cream herself when she opens the gift and, when her inevitable divorce ensues, she might remember . . . and screw you.

894. Another man may touch your genitals on just two occasions:

    (1) When he is a doctor and it is your annual physical

    (2) When he is an Indian, you are dead, and your wagon train on the Oregon Trail has just been ransacked

895. If a horror movie has truly made you too scared to sleep alone but you are afraid of being made fun of by your roommates, a man may pretend to have fallen asleep while reading and leave the light on.

896. Only black men can successfully pull off the "I'm balding, so I'm going to shave my head" gambit. For his inexplicable ability to turn male pattern baldness into a cool trait for black men, every time a bald black man has sex, he should mail Michael Jordan a check for $20.

897. If you have a personal sex toy other than your palm, you're trying way too hard.

898. Even if you can't fix a car or if it's not even broken, always have a body-shop dolly you can slide under a car with (not a skateboard) in your open garage. Don a wife-beater or cuttoffs (not jeans). When girls walk by from class, roll yourself in and out a few times and pick up random tools. Hit stuff. Make noise. Scream "Fuckin' Hemi!" Empty beer cans are a bonus. Have

extra oil handy for added grime. The next day, start the car when they walk by. Ask if they need a ride. Note: Works best in the Deep South.

899. If your dog has a spiked collar, that's awesome. If you have one that's gay. Really gay.

900. Guns are for cowards. Next time you want to inflict bodily harm, use a crossbow. If someone can't avoid the arrow, he deserves it for whatever he did. Be sure to aim below the waist, to avoid attempted murder charges.

901. Regardless of your destination, if you are traveling more than fifty miles from home, pack a swimsuit and be prepared to "jacuzzi."

902. Think about, and commit to memory, how you would hunt, capture, and ultimately kill squirrel, or similar small game. If the world is wrought with cataclysmic drought/famine/plague/war, etc., and only you, a hot woman, and another man are left on the squelched earth, do not doubt that said hot woman will swear allegiance (and her corresponding sexual consort) to the man who can provide her with consistent nourishment. Consider constructing a loose patch of leaves with a nut placed in the middle, covering a pit of poison-tipped spikes.

903. If you break up with a girlfriend and the two of you in happier times had adopted a cat, fight for custody

of the cat as if your life depended on it. If you are victorious in this life-or-death struggle, immediately donate said cat to the Humane Society.

904. If you are ever on a televised talk show, you must be drunk.

905. Dogs and potbellied pigs are the only pets allowed on leashes. Or if your pet can maul someone and/or is on the endangered species list, a leash is recommended. Addendum: If you ever see a man not in the AARP walking a cat on a leash, by law, you are required to let loose any pet you own from said "mauling" category above.

906. If you are in a dark theater sitting down with someone, it had better be a movie. Suggestion: If you see people in tuxes, the word *intermission*, or have to be quiet, turn quickly and run. It is not a movie theater.

907. For every picture in your wallet, you must have a condom, cigarette paper, or throwing star.

908. Give everyone you have known for longer than two days some sort of nickname. This will help you look like you actually remember his or her name.

909. If you do not have to go to work that day, showering and shaving are completely optional. In fact, shaving is frowned upon even if you go to work.

910. When racing go-carts, victory is less important than who causes the most spectacular crash. Also, the person who forces the workers to come out the most times and push a buddy off the guardrail so he can drive again, is the winner.

911. If you've ever owned a DVD that stars Hugh Grant, you are a woman. The only way to cure this is to douse the DVD in lighter fluid and set it on fire while masturbating to a picture of Kobe Tai.

912. When your girlfriend comes to you and says, "The computer doctor says my computer stopped running because of all the porn viruses," you have no idea how such a thing could have happened.

913. If you have the ability to sing well, you should use this gift whenever around a group of women. If you can, sing a sad and lonely melody while shedding a single tear and staring off into the distance. (Note: It is not normally acceptable to even fake-cry, but an exception is made if you are doing it to get laid. Real crying while singing is not acceptable.)

914. At some point in your life, you will find yourself in a legitimate whorehouse. You may find this incomprehensible and think we're joking. We're not. Do not, we repeat, do not, allow them to open bottles for you. That shit's expensive.

915. Anytime you are in serious danger of getting your ass kicked, punch a guy in the balls and run. There is no shame in this. Well, okay, there's shame, but not as much shame as getting your head rammed into a concrete floor forty-eight times.

916. Before you hire a stripper for a bachelor party, make sure she doesn't have young children. Nothing kills a night like milk squirting out of a stripper's tits while you're titty-fucking her with a strap-on dildo.

917. Everyone has a friend who gets carried away when the stripper is visiting and attempts to lick the stripper's pussy. Never, ever, allow this man to share your drink. Your buddy has just done the rough equivalent of sucking 438 cocks, 237 of which will have been infected with VD. Nice move.

918. The girls at amusement parks who wear bikini tops will show you their tits for a discreetly handed-over dollar. Or if not yet, they will within a year.

919. When not at work, answer all phone calls with, "What?" and end all calls by abruptly hanging up at the end of a sentence.

920. If you are ever in prison, remember the following guidelines: If another prisoner tries to steal your cornbread, you should punch and stomp him repeatedly. If he tries to steal your meat, you should shank him. If he tries to give you his "meat," you should have

him killed, but make sure you have someone from a rival gang do it for you, thus leaving you in the clear, as most people in jail are probably a lot tougher than you.

921. If something happens to the pilot, you must land the plane.

922. Always have an object within two feet that is tossable. (Definition of *tossable*: an item used to throw up and down repeatedly, hypnotizing a man to completely tune out all ambient stimulation, e.g., a football, tennis ball, ball of paper, lightbulb.)

923. Be careful about making fun of seemingly gay men. As much as it pains you to admit it, Ricky Martin could probably kick your ass.

924. If you have ever felt even a glimmer of doubt before donning a wife-beater to leave your house, then you are not man enough to wear it.

925. The ability to twirl a pen in one hand without dropping it is a skill to be revered by all men.

926. If you have a tattoo on your lower back, it better damn well be connected to the one on your upper back.

927. There is straight and there is gay. There is no such thing as metrosexual.

928. If you join a lodge-style club that requires its members to wear an animal head at meetings, then you are awesome.

929. When driving behind an emergency vehicle on a high-speed freeway, feel free to tail along as if you are involved in the rescue as well. Simulate using a walkie-talkie to call for backup. Passing an ambulance is perfectly fine. Passing a speeding police car, however, is not recommended.

930. Shortening words to one syllable, such as *fav* or *rad*, is glaring evidence that your testes have not descended.

931. A true man cannot decide between steak and sex, unless you are Morgan Freeman, in which case you eat steak while having sex.

932. If a man insists on wearing a ponytail, insist on riding him like an equine. Jump on his back and attempt to put a bit with reins in his mouth. If there is no bit available, a number two pencil with string on both ends is an acceptable substitute. He will most likely try to buck you off. Tame him with your spurs.

933. The word *hymen* is always fun to use. Sprinkle it liberally into conversation if your buddy insists on talking to fat chicks. Accept that the phrase, "I bet you'd even eat a hymen," represents a guaranteed way to never have to speak to a fat chick again.

934. A man may have a garden only if he grows food to eat and occasionally slaps other men in the face with the ears of corn from his garden.

935. If you live in the suburbs and have found yourself competing with other men about grass, shrubbery, who has the best paving job, or whose wisteria vines are climbing faster on the wainscott, do everyone a favor and file for divorce. She will get to keep the house but this is a small price to pay for your dignity.

936. When spending the day on a boat, a man can bring the following: a Frisbee, beer, and his swimsuit. Anything more is just showing off.

937. If ever an uncomfortable silence falls between two men, this unbearably awkward moment can be broken by sounding off in one of the three following ways:

(1) "Did you see that [insert sport here] game last night? [Insert player's name] was playing out of his head!"

(2) "That [insert hot actress's name here] has a great set of chest midgets, doesn't she? I'd like to wake up with her face between my legs."

(3) Farting.

938. Somebody calls 900 sex numbers or else there wouldn't be five million in existence. Even if this has caused

you to run up $20K in credit card debt, you have no idea who these men are.

939. When about to be sodomized against your will in jail, cut your losses. Ask for a little romance first. This will be the last time you are raped. He's not gonna buy the cow if he can get the milk for free.

940. If a man does not know what a safety, sacrifice fly, or donkey punch is, you cannot be friends with him.

941. Sometimes, having to go to the bathroom hurts very badly . . . like, you almost cannot walk. Not being able to walk properly is a disability or handicap. Thus, you may use the handicapped stall with a clear conscience.

942. If you ever attend a party thrown by another man and there are more than three candles burning, feel free to burn his place down and leave.

943. Every time you see a wonder of nature (e.g., the Grand Canyon, Niagara Falls, etc.) you should pee on it, thus staking your claim to it in the true man's fashion.

944. If you are dating a girl with excruciatingly hot roommates, feel free to accidentally (on purpose) see them at any time scantily clad. As an added bonus, fantasize about their joining in on the next rogering session, during the actual rogering session with your girlfriend. It will make the sex better for her, and inevitably she will brag to her roommates. They will

be impressed at your sexual prowess, giving them a mental bookmark just in case you guys ever break up. See, everybody wins.

945. Under no circumstances admit to bathing with your father when you were a child. If there are pictures, destroy them.

946. When playing blackjack with your friends and someone chooses to hit on sixteen and subsequently busts, it is always funny to pick up your drink and say, "Thirty-two" in mock salute. If your friend hits on seventeen, you need to gamble more often.

947. If you ever see a man out in public wearing one of those charm necklaces that has candies on it, squeal, rush forward, push your own hand behind his neck, and continue pulling him lower until his face meets your knee.

948. You have no idea why your girlfriend's Victoria's Secret catalog has sticky pages.

949. If you have tiled or wooden floors in your house/apartment, here is a good way to measure when to clean: if you don't leave footprints when you walk through the room, you are safe for another week.

950. Gay men are not to be feared; they are your allies because they can say and ask anything sexual to a hot woman and the woman will laugh.

951. If you borrow $20 from a friend whom you have known for over five years, then you don't need to re-pay him. Simply say something along the lines of, "I'll buy the first couple of rounds this weekend" or "I'll pay for the next Mexican male whore in Guadalajara."

952. When assigning a nickname to a male friend, the cardinal rule is that it should be embarrassing. For instance, if you find out that a friend's parents used to call him "Claybobedubinstein" as a child, then "Steiner" is an appropriate nickname. (Clay didn't know this one was making the book.)

953. Accept that the greatest three-word chant ever created is "Show your tits." Use it liberally and with pride.

954. When queried, you must confess to the least sexy visual image you have ever utilized to masturbate. But only one.

955. If you own a book called *The Idiot's Guide to . . .* or *. . . for Dummies*, then you are a complete asshole. Why the hell did you buy that?

956. Preferring Low-Limit Hold'em to No-Limit Hold'em is akin to being the small English boy in the following exchange:

> DAD: SON, don't you think it's time you learned how to ride a two-wheel bike?

SMALL ENGLISH BOY: No, father, please do not remove my training wheels. I so enjoy the security and sense of well-being they provide.

957. If you call a man a "bitch," be prepared to kill and devour him or alternatively to be killed and or be devoured.

958. Find all locations within your workplace where it is possible to do pull-ups. Rep them out whenever a woman is present.

959. If you are wearing an article of clothing that your three-year-old niece describes as "pretty," take it off immediately, set it on fire, then douse the fire with day-old, flat Coors Light. (Note: You must not open a new Coors Light to put out the fire, as it is forbidden to waste drinkable beer.)

960. Every man should have a library of Arnold Schwarzenegger movie quotes memorized and readily available to be applied in any life situation, fully equipped with your best Arnold impersonation. Examples of some such quotes would include: "He was a hothead," "If you're going to do it, do it now!" "It's not a tumor," or, after impaling someone with a large hunting knife to a dry-erase board . . . "Stick around."

961. Despite what your girlfriend or wife has told you, every scented candle smells pretty much the same . . . like your masculinity burning.

962. If you manage to successfully record yourself giving someone a cock-stache as a prank, feel free to celebrate, but not until you control all copies of the film.

963. Learn several ways to tie a tie. Conversely, you only need to learn one way to remove a girl's panties from under her skirt.

964. There is no time or age moratorium on certain jokes, once puberty has been passed. For instance, if your friend wore a Mickey Mouse shirt with matching shorts after his voice had changed, he may be ridiculed mercilessly until his death . . . or until he kills you.

965. If you are unable to open a jar and someone else does it for you, instead of saying, "I loosened it for you," just smash it on the table and slit your throat with the shards.

966. Eating hot foods is a must. Whenever eating at a restaurant that serves spicy dishes, you should order the hottest item on the menu, then tell everyone, "This isn't that hot, it's really good actually," ignoring the fact that it is eating through your tracheal wall and will leave you shitting liquid hot lava the next morning.

967. Pee in public at least once in every city you visit.

968. If you have never fired a gun, you are not a man. If you have shot a gun on more than five separate occasions, you are either in law enforcement, in the military, or on parole.

969. Riding a motorcycle is basically the stupidest thing you can do with your life. Do this at every available opportunity.

970. When driving, if a friend passes you, accelerate. Force him into oncoming traffic if necessary. Just don't let him beat you.

971. If someone in the car changes the radio to an easy listening or soft rock station, turn the radio off to demonstrate how much better silence is than Kenny G.

972. Treat all overly friendly men with total hostility until it is clear they are not trying to have sex with you. Sufficient evidence of nonhomosexuality includes arm-wrestling, crushing beer cans on your head, and accurate use of the words *poonhound* and *muffdive*.

973. If you are married and go house-shopping, buy something less than you can afford. When your wife gets banged by your gardener and files for divorce, this will make her getting to keep the house seem less painful.

974. It's time for men to bring back the hot girl whistle. Next time a hot girl walks past you, whistle. Incidentally, all whistling outside of the presence of hot women is punishable by hanging.

975. At the STD clinic, when they tell you, "Don't worry, this will feel just like a beesting," worry. They mean a beesting inside your pee hole.

Index